D1545600

The Spontaneous Gesture

The Spontaneous Gesture ੬ఌ

SELECTED LETTERS OF
D. W. WINNICOTT

EDITED BY

F. Robert Rodman

HARVARD UNIVERSITY PRESS
CAMBRIDGE, MASSACHUSETTS
AND LONDON, ENGLAND
1987

Library of Congress Cataloging-in-Publication Data

Winnicott, D. W. (Donald Woods), 1896–1971.
    The spontaneous gesture.

    Includes index.
    1. Winnicott, D. W. (Donald Woods), 1896–1971—
Correspondence. 2. Psychoanalysts—Great Britain—
Correspondence. 3. Psychoanalysis. 4. Child psychiatry.
I. Rodman, F. Robert (Francis Robert).
II. Title. [DNLM: 1. Personality Development—
correspondence. 2. Psychoanalytic Theory—
correspondence. wz 100w776s]
RC509.W56   1987   616.89′17′0924   86-18483
ISBN 0-674-83336-8 (alk. paper)

For Sarah, my daughter

and in memory of my mother, Sarah Frieda Rodman

Contents

Illustrations

Preface

I HAD NO WAY of knowing that publication of the letters of
D. W. Winnicott was being planned when, in 1979, I wrote to Dr.
Winnicott's widow, Mrs. Clare Winnicott, and asked whether I
might edit them. I had just reread his response to a paper I had
sent him in 1969. In its length and openness, his letter was more
than a reply; it was a gift. It seemed likely that many other corre-
spondents had been so favored. Winnicott's work, and, I suppose,
Winnicott himself, had always seemed highly accessible to me,
from my first reading of him as a medical student. And so the act
of mailing him a paper without asking in advance whether he
would mind was as typical of how I felt about him as was the letter
I sent ten years later to Mrs. Winnicott, something out of the blue
that might be acceptable anyway. It was.

I went to her home in Lower Belgrave Street in May of 1980
to meet with her and with Ray Shepherd, a psychoanalyst and
a member of the Winnicott Publications Committee, and Peter
Tizard, Winnicott's old friend and distinguished fellow pediatrician. After dinner, Mrs. Winnicott showed me to the comfortable
basement room where the letters were kept. They had been organized in a series of ring binders from 1958 onward, one per year,
with all the correspondence alphabetized. There were also several
boxes full of unsorted letters and miscellaneous documents. I
scanned this material and became convinced that a great deal of it
would be of interest to a wide readership of psychoanalysts and
others of diverse background.

The following year I arranged to have the material copied. But
it was not until 1984 that I could continue the necessary work, and
by then Mrs. Winnicott had succumbed to the illness that she had

struggled against for many years. She had considered at length what to do with the Winnicott documents, and had decided to send the originals to the library of the New York Hospital-Cornell Medical Center for safekeeping and future scholarship, with duplicates to be available in England at the Wellcome Institute for the History of Medicine. Long before, she had made careful arrangements for the editing and publishing of her husband's work through a board of editors consisting of herself, Madeleine Davis, and Ray Shepherd. After her death, Christopher Bollas became the third member. Later another trove of letters was discovered, and from it a large number were added to the earlier collection.

In all, about 825 letters written by Winnicott survive. For this book I have chosen only those with a direct bearing on his work and theories. Letters before 1949 are sparse. He probably lacked secretarial help before then. In those times as well he passed through a personal upheaval, which included his father's death, divorce from his first wife, and, in 1951, remarriage. Records may have been lost or discarded. A move to new living and working quarters in Chester Square marked the beginning of that final score of years in which his genius was widely recognized. Perhaps at that point he began to realize that a more complete record of his correspondence would one day be of interest, to himself at least and possibly to others.

The letters in this book are, with two exceptions, taken from typed, unsigned copies that Winnicott kept. Letter 1, to his sister, is from a photocopy of the handwritten letter, and for letter 118, to me, I have the typed original. Complete letters appear wherever possible. Deletions have been made primarily to protect confidences, and for the same reason capital letters have been substituted for a few names. Deletions are indicated by ellipsis dots and emendations by square brackets. A few simple errors in spelling and punctuation have been corrected without note.

Acknowledgments

I AM DEEPLY GRATEFUL to the late Mrs. Clare Winnicott, who entrusted me with the task of editing these letters. Her warm, witty, and intelligent presence is sorely missed.

Madeleine Davis took up this project where Mrs. Winnicott left off and has been a helpful and stimulating guide throughout. Her wide knowledge and, more than that, her grasp of the true value of Winnicott's work and life are enormous. She has given me much information and good advice. Ray Shepherd has been a source of quiet encouragement from the very beginning. Through his inquiries at the archives of the British Psychoanalytic Society, I have been able to identify the dates and titles of most of the papers to which Winnicott responds in these letters.

Arthur Rosenthal, director of Harvard University Press, responded with enthusiasm to the proposal to publish the letters. He had been well acquainted with Winnicott and his writings as publisher of his *Collected Papers* at Basic Books.

My good friend Lance Lee gave me the benefit of his incisive understanding of Winnicott's work, and, as usual, sage comments on writing, this time on the organization of the Introduction.

My wife and children tolerated a lengthy absorption with Winnicott, the hours in front of the word processor, and the moods that accompany the preparation of a book. I love them for that and for everything else.

Introduction

D. W. WINNICOTT was one of the major figures in British psychoanalysis in the generation following Freud. His writings were primarily concerned with the nature of relationships, beginning with that of mother and infant, which he described with great subtlety. As a member of the British Middle Group, he stood apart from the clusters around Melanie Klein and Anna Freud, lending heart to those of a similarly independent bent and, at the same time, forming a tenuous bridge between the two rival factions. The many psychoanalytic books and papers that make reference to his work attest both to the enduring value of his ideas and to their capacity to enrich and facilitate the thinking of others. Because his writings retain freshness and the capacity to stimulate unexpected inference, his influence has continued to grow with the years.

Donald Woods Winnicott was born in 1896 in Plymouth, Devon, a stronghold of the nonconformist Wesleyan tradition. His father, a successful and much-admired merchant and mayor of the town, was knighted for civic work. Donald was the youngest of three, with two elder sisters, and apparently had a happy childhood. At fourteen, he left home for the Leys School in Cambridge, where the following year, while being treated for a broken collarbone, he decided to become a doctor. Much taken with Darwin's ideas, he studied biology at Jesus College, Cambridge, and then medicine at St. Bartholomew's Hospital in London. In medical school, he converted to the Anglican Church.[1] Also while a

1. Personal communication, Clare Winnicott.

medical student, he found himself unable to recall his dreams and, while looking for a book that might help him, came across a work on Freud by a Swiss parson named Oskar Pfister. This introduced Winnicott to psychoanalytic writings.[2]

Winnicott served as Surgeon-Probationer on a destroyer for a time during the First World War. He resumed the study of medicine and qualified in 1920. In 1923 he married.

Also in 1923, he became physician to the Paddington Green Children's Hospital, a post he held until 1963. His Wednesday clinics, which gradually evolved from traditional pediatrics to child psychiatry, were part of the continuity of his medical experience, which amounted eventually to about 60,000 cases. In 1923 as well he started a ten-year analysis with James Strachey. This decade was a period of great change for the British Psycho-Analytical Society. In 1926, Melanie Klein moved from Berlin to London, brought by Ernest Jones for the immediate purpose of analyzing his wife and two children. A conflict between Klein and Anna Freud in matters of theory and the technique of child analysis had begun in earnest and was to be one of the principal topics of conversation for many years to come. In 1933, the discussions of scientific matters in the British Society were much affected by the vituperative attacks on Melanie Klein by Edward Glover and his analysand Melitta Schmideberg, Klein's daughter, who accused her mother of "trying to force feelings into me."

In 1935, Winnicott began six years of supervision with Mrs. Klein. He wanted to be analyzed by her, but this would have made it impossible for him to do what she wished: to analyze her son under her supervision. He refused this arrangement, but did become her son's analyst from 1935 to 1939.[3] In the late 1930s, Winnicott undertook a second analysis with Joan Riviere.

Freud arrived in London on June 6, 1938, at a time when the membership of the British Society was fully one-third of Central European origin. After Freud's death in September of 1939, and with the war raging, the British Society fell into divisive quarrel-

2. "A Personal View: 10, Donald Winnicott." *St. Mary's Hospital Gazette* 67, no. 5 (July-August 1961).

3. Phyllis Grosskurth, *Melanie Klein: Her World and Her Work* (New York: Knopf, 1986).

ing. The so-called Controversial Discussions of the early 1940s were an attempt at finding a solution. A split between followers of Klein and of Anna Freud, which would have led to the formation of a second psychoanalytic society, was staved off by an arrangement that provided for two programs of training. Unwilling to align himself with either the A Group (the Kleinians) or the B Group (Anna Freud's followers), Winnicott joined what came to be known as the Middle Groupers, which included Michael Balint, Ronald Fairbairn, Sylvia Payne, Ella Sharpe, and Marjorie Brierley. This decision fitted the person who would later add the term "transitional object" to our vocabulary, and who would concentrate his writings on the area between people, the locus of relating and of cultural experience, where motion and play are the characteristic features.

Simultaneous with the events of wartime, Winnicott became consultant psychiatrist in the scheme to evacuate children from London to the countryside. This took him to Oxfordshire, where he supervised the treatment of runaways and delinquents and developed his ideas on the subject of "the antisocial tendency." On this project he worked with Clare Britton, a psychiatric social worker who would later become his second wife. After the death of his beloved father in 1948, he moved toward divorce, and then in 1951 he remarried. In this period he brought forth the paper for which he is most famous, "Transitional Objects and Transitional Phenomena."[4] This work, which had been foreshadowed by his 1945 paper "Primitive Emotional Development,"[5] ushered in the creative final twenty years of his life, during which a steady contribution of original ideas challenged and deepened the course of psychoanalytic thought. The long-term effects of his writings are yet to be seen. He died in 1971.

Among the many posts Winnicott held were these: physician in charge of the Child Department of the British Psycho-Analytical Institute for twenty-five years and president for two three-year terms (1956–59 and 1965–68). He was also scientific secretary and training secretary for three-year terms. He was chairman of the

4. In *Collected Papers: Through Pediatrics to Psychoanalysis* (1958; London: Hogarth Press, 1982) and in *Playing and Reality* (London: Tavistock, 1971).
5. In *Collected Papers*.

Medical Section of the British Psychological Society, president of
the Paediatric Section of the Royal Society of Medicine, president
of the Association of Child Psychology and Psychiatry. There
were many honorary memberships, consultantships, and invited
lectureships. He was in great demand as a lecturer to psychoanalytic and lay groups, and gave a highly regarded series of BBC
broadcasts about child development. Many books flowed from his
pen, beginning with a textbook of pediatrics in 1931,[6] when he
was the first to introduce analytic ideas to the practice of pediatrics. He wrote for both psychoanalytic and lay audiences. His considerable unpublished work is finally becoming available just now.

I saw Winnicott only once, at a meeting of the British Society
in 1963, when he read "Communicating and Non-communicating
Leading to a Study of Certain Opposites."[7] In this paper he argued
that there is a part of every person that does not wish to be
known. "At the centre of each person is an incommunicado element, and this is sacred and most worthy of preservation . . . We
can understand the hatred people have of psycho-analysis which
has penetrated a long way into the human personality, and which
provides a threat to the human individual in his need to be secretly
isolated. The question is: how to be isolated without having to be
insulated?" One might have taken this to refer to that state of self-
investment which Freud thought was there at the beginning, primary narcissism (this is how Anna Freud interpreted it),[8] or to a
continuation throughout life of the same phenomenon. Yet Winnicott's idea does not quite belong under that heading. In another
paper he insists that the innermost core "must never be affected by
external reality."[9] And in a letter to Melanie Klein (17 November
1952) he remarks of a colleague, "if he were growing a daffodil he
would think that he was making the daffodil out of a bulb instead
of enabling the bulb to develop into a daffodil by good enough

---

6. *Clinical Notes on Disorders in Childhood* (London: Heinemann, 1931).
7. In *The Maturational Processes and the Facilitating Environment* (New York: International Universities Press, 1965).
8. Personal communication, 1963.
9. "Classification: Is There a Psycho-Analytic Contribution to Psychiatric Classification?" in *The Maturational Processes and the Facilitating Environment*.

nurture." To a correspondent in Tanzania he says of children, "We cannot even teach them to walk, but their innate tendency to walk at a certain age needs us as supporting figures . . ."[10] He seems to be saying that just as the genetic-organic underpinnings of physical life must be left intact if they are to manifest themselves properly, so too in the life of the mind what we do as parents—or as analysts of deeply disturbed patients—is to provide proper conditions for growth. In leaving out the term narcissism, he opens up the subject. He does not invade or take possession of the territory to which he refers by the use of a metapsychological term. A touch of wonder remains when we think of the inviolate bulb.

Winnicott carefully guarded his own sensitivity.

> I am reminded of a curious thing about myself right back in the twenties. After being an Out-patient Physician at Paddington Green I became entitled to beds. This was very exciting, because the doctor in charge of cases in the hospital has status. Having beds means that one has arrived. Hardly knowing why, I refused to step up. I got permission to use beds where necessary but I handed the in-patients over to my junior. I knew at the time why I was doing this. I said to myself: the distress of babies and small children in a hospital ward, even a very nice one, adds up to something terrific. Going into the wards disturbs me very much. If I become an in-patient doctor I shall develop the capacity not to be disturbed by the distress of the children, otherwise I shall not be able to be an effective doctor. I will therefore concentrate on my O.P. work and avoid becoming callous in order to be efficient.[11]

In addition to "not taking beds," it was typical of him that, throughout a long career as a pediatrician and writer of books about child development for the lay public, he would not consent to offer direct advice, believing that "the baby has a relationship with the mother and father that develops according to what all three are like, and although it is possible to talk about what happens and to say how one thing may be better than another, the thing is how it works out naturally, and not whether it is right or wrong according to some standard statement."[12] He had found

10. To J. D. Collinson, 10 March 1969.
11. To Margaret Torrie, 5 September 1967.
12. To Marjorie Spence, 23 November 1967.

early on that the physical examination contributed little to his psychiatric consultations with children, and gave it up as an inflexible routine, though he maintained throughout his career that physical examinations were indispensable to pediatric practice. Psychoanalysis, he later said, could be considered an extension of history-taking. At one point, he decided also to stop prescribing medications.

This pattern of restraint, which amounted to an exquisite form of respect, was intended to reduce interference with the process of observing. Psychoanalysis, with its abstinence by both patient and analyst, both being required to behave according to strict rules, must have been crucial in reinforcing this side of him. In discussing his theory of the transitional object, he speaks of the paradox of its origin, that it is both found and created. He warns that this paradox must be respected "and not solved by a restatement that, by its cleverness, seems to eliminate the paradox."[13] His term "impingement" denotes the tendency of certain mothers to interfere with the going-on-being of their infants by unnecessary intrusions, thereby hindering their natural unfolding. Not only did he strive to eliminate any impingement by himself on his patients, but his own development must have shown him that he must not tolerate the adult equivalent of impingement on himself and, even more, that he and others needed a tolerant atmosphere (not necessarily an uncritical one) for the emergence of what he called gestures. He could understand the needs of anyone with an original idea.

In the 1952 letter to Melanie Klein, he discusses her lack of response to a paper he had presented:[14] "What I was wanting on Friday undoubtedly was that there should be some move from your direction towards the gesture that I make in this paper. It is a creative gesture and I cannot make any relationship through this gesture except if someone come to meet it. I think that I was wanting something which I have no right to expect from your group, and it is really of the nature of a therapeutic act, something which I could not get in either of my two long analyses, although I got

13. "Communicating and Not Communicating Leading to a Study of Certain Opposites."
14. "Anxiety Associated with Insecurity," in *Collected Papers*.

so much else." He goes on to speak of the need to keep psycho-analytic language alive through making room for ideas from diverse sources, expressed in the language of each contributor. "The initial statement is usually made at great cost and for some time afterwards the man or woman who has done this work is in a sensitive state as he is personally involved."

Not surprisingly, the content of Winnicott's personal striving is echoed in his conceptualizations. His theory of development delineates the conditions under which the infant's maturational processes meet with a facilitating environment, so that those processes reach full development and make for pleasure and creativity. His theory of health is not defined as the absence of pathology. He is interested in more than that. He wants to define a healthy life in positive terms.[15]

Winnicott's insistence on being himself was more evident than for most analysts. He came up against a number of barriers in the British Society, of which the two leaders from the late 1930s were Anna Freud and Melanie Klein. Since he had been part of the Kleinian contingent during the Controversial Discussions that led to a division of training, Miss Freud had reason to consider him an adversary. A letter in which he criticized a presentation by one of her followers caused a furor in the early 1950s. But she could change her mind. She responded to a 1961 review of Winnicott's *Collected Papers* by indicating that it was the first time she had understood his theories and his therapeutic intentions. She told Winnicott in 1968 that his concept of the transitional object had "conquered the analytic world."[16] And earlier she had recalled in a letter to him that after the Freuds moved to London he was the only member of the British Society who called at their Maresfield Gardens home to ask if they were all right.[17] Nevertheless, the letters attest to a formal distance between Winnicott and Anna Freud.

His relations with Melanie Klein and the Kleinians were another matter. Klein had been his mentor in the late 1930s, and he valued

15. "Creativity and Its Origins," in *The Maturational Processes and the Facilitating Environment.*
16. Anna Freud to Winnicott, 30 October 1968.
17. Anna Freud to Winnicott, 15 February 1949.

her ideas for the rest of his life, in spite of all disagreements. He regarded hers as the most creative mind in psychoanalysis, after Freud's. He analyzed her son, though not, as she had requested, under her supervision. In the early days, she wrote him long, affectionate letters. In time he came to disagree with a number of her theories, especially elaborations on the death instinct, such as constitutional envy. He objected especially to the way her ideas were put forth. In letter after letter, he tried to convince the Kleinians that they were sealing themselves off from others by their use of code-words. He deeply believed in the value of Klein's earlier theories, and thought they were being ignored because of the way they were being presented. Eventually, he saw that Klein herself had much to do with this spirit. His objections settled especially on her unwillingness to acknowledge the importance of the actual mother and her actual behavior in the development of the infant. As a pediatrician with a vast experience he could not help being rooted in the empirical reality of early infant development. This aspect of his knowledge perfectly complemented what he was learning in child analysis and in the process of reconstructing the early life of deeply disturbed adult patients.

The role of external reality was brought into question by Freud's discovery that reports of sexual molestation in childhood usually were the result of Oedipal fantasies rather than actual events. This opened the world of fantasy to careful study and launched Freud on his great work of demonstrating that a person's instinctual urges and infantile neurosis color and shape the course of life. This point of view, which might be regarded as the backbone of psychoanalytic theory and therapy, has been repeatedly challenged. Klein probably represents its apotheosis. By virtually excluding external reality from a formative role in development, her theory achieves the impression that the technique it generates will benefit the patient through shattering insights. Winnicott, firmly rooted in the psychoanalytic tradition but also a practical observer of children and their parents in distress, could bring in external reality as an influence without sacrificing the significance of the child's fantasy life in the process. His own sense of reality, perhaps even his sense of fairness, demanded it of him.

His books for parents, his BBC broadcasts, his teaching of social workers at the London School of Economics, his role as a most respected pediatrician—all made him a public spokesman when important issues arose. In his public letters, we see the balance between his observation of and participation in external reality, on the one hand, and his close focus on the inner reality of his patients, on the other.

He went on developing his own ideas, but not without an opposition that became insidious. A letter (3 February 1956) to his second analyst, Joan Riviere, begins:

> After Mrs. Klein's paper you and she spoke to me and within the framework of friendliness you gave me to understand that both of you are absolutely certain that there is no positive contribution to be made from me to the interesting attempt Melanie is making all the time to state the psychology of the earliest stages. You will agree that you implied that the trouble is that I am unable to recognize that Melanie does say the very things that I am asking her to say. In other words, there is a block in me.

He goes on: "I want you to know that I do not accept what you and Melanie implied, namely that my concern about Melanie's statement of the psychology of earliest infancy is based on subjective rather than objective factors."

Even if Winnicott's theories were related to his own conflicts, it would have been a mistake to regard them as invalid on that account. He certainly could not have replied to such accusations in kind. Riviere had the advantage of having analyzed him, while he did not have the corresponding one of knowing the intimate details of Melanie Klein's childhood. Anyone's theories stand on their own, of course, to be confirmed or refuted, however interesting or even neurotic their origins may be. Attempts at devaluing ideas by ad hominem references to unanalyzed conflict are hardly unknown in the public and private deliberations of psychoanalysts of various schools. But we rarely have a chance to identify such instances in written form, or in cases such as that of Winnicott, in which a deliberate effort is made to crush potentially major contributions.

The struggle is most ardently expressed in Winnicott's 1952 letter to Klein. She had invited him to contribute a chapter to her

forthcoming book, and he was explaining why he could not. Joan
Riviere had written a preface to the book in which she claimed
that Klein "has in fact produced something new in psychoanalysis:
namely, an *integrated* theory which, though still in outline, nevertheless takes account of all psychical manifestations, normal and
abnormal, from birth to death, and leaves no unbridgeable gulfs
and no phenomena outstanding without intelligible relation to the
rest."[18] Winnicott wrote to Klein:

> I personally think that it is very important that your work should be
> restated by people discovering in their own way and presenting what
> they discover in their own language. It is only in this way that the
> language will be kept alive. If you make the stipulation that in future
> only your language shall be used for the statement of other people's
> discoveries then the language becomes a dead language, as it has al-
> ready become in the Society . . . I am concerned with this set-up
> which might be called Kleinian which I believe to be the real danger
> to the diffusion of your work. Your ideas will only live in so far as they
> are rediscovered and reformulated by original people in the psycho-
> analytic movement and outside it . . . The danger is . . . that the co-
> terie develops a system based on the defence of the position gained by
> the original worker, in this case yourself . . . You are the only one who
> can destroy this language called the Kleinian doctrine and Kleinism
> and all that with a constructive aim. If you do not destroy it then this
> artificially integrated phenomenon must be attacked destructively. It
> invites attack, and as I tried to point out, Mrs. Riviere's unfortunate
> sentence in her otherwise excellent introduction puts the matter ex-
> actly into words which can be quoted by people who are not neces-
> sarily the enemies of your ideas but who are the enemies of systems.

When Winnicott says "If you do not destroy it then this artificially integrated phenomenon must be attacked destructively," he
welds together two aspects of his character: the long effort to har-
ness his own aggression for constructive purposes, and his religious side. In objecting to dogma in the psychoanalytic endeavor,
he is recommending obedience to the Second Commandment.

The word "ruthless" would, at first glance, not seem appropriate for a gentle person such as Winnicott, one whose reputation

---

18. Joan Riviere, Preface, in Melanie Klein et al., *Developments in Psycho-Analysis*
    (London: Hogarth Press, 1952).

as a clinician is one of consummate intuition and care. Yet this was an adjective that was heard on two occasions at the memorial meeting in his honor at the British Society.[19] He could be ruthless where a matter of principle was involved, and he wrote a good deal about ruthlessness as a stage of infant development[20] and about reaching that stage in the analysis of very disturbed patients.[21] In his role as an officer of the British Society, he was always on the initiative. In the letters, when he is critical he is often unflinchingly frontal. The sense of honest, well-meant criticism is sometimes enhanced by statements of friendly feeling, but there are some letters with very little of that.

One of his early papers, "Hate in the Counter-Transference,"[22] opened the door for the use of that powerful word, *hate,* in the relations of analysts to patients. Around the time of that paper he wrote the author of a bill to socialize medicine in Britain: "I must . . . be honest with myself and express to you yourself the hate that rises naturally in me . . ."[23] In a letter about sponsored television he says: "I know I shall hate politicians with increasing hatred as I gradually see a new generation growing up taking for granted the advertisers' right to intrude."[24] Citing "the advertisers' right to intrude" as the reason for his hatred is characteristic of one who called our attention to the inmost core of the individual, where no one is welcome. In a letter to the periodical *New Society* (23 March 1964), he comments on social work of all kinds, including psychoanalysis: "the worker's hate is contained in the structure of the professional relationship, its finite nature, its being paid for etc. etc." Hate not only emerges sometimes in treating certain patients, but is an everyday part of the work. In "The Use of an Object,"[25] one of his last papers, Winnicott's struggle to state the constructive use of the destructive impulse led him to demonstrate

---

19. "Remarks by Mrs. Marion Milner" and "Remarks by Dr. W. H. Gillespie," *British Psycho-Analytical Society and the Institute of Psycho-Analysis Scientific Bulletin*, no. 57, 1972.

20. "The Depressive Position in Normal Emotional Development," in *Collected Papers*.

21. To Barbara Lantos, 8 November 1956.

22. In *Collected Papers*.

23. To Lord Beveridge, 15 October 1946.

24. To the *Times*, 21 July 1954.

25. In *Playing and Reality*.

how the sense of reality depends upon surviving constant attempts to destory the object. He presents the idea that a person becomes of use to another, becomes more real, by surviving the ongoing aggressive aspect of a relationship.

He regarded sentimentality as a weakness to be guarded against. That is to say, natural aggression must be given its due. This is most evident in his letters on the subject of delinquency. "A sentimental swing toward the antisocial child or adult must sooner or later be followed by a reaction."[26] "My idea is that any kind of sentimentality is worse than useless."[27] In the *New Society* letter he says: ". . . there is great danger in a dissemination of a sentimental idea about psychoanalysis, social work, or being a parent." In a letter to the *Observer* (12 October 1964), speaking of mothers of infants, he says: "I have brought in the word *devotion* here at risk, because there are some who associate this word with sentimentality." A sentimental idea is one that leaves no room for hate, or at least for aggression. Commenting on a proposed translation of his paper on transitional objects into French, he says: "The word 'tender' is rather good but it emphasizes an absence of aggression and destruction whereas the word 'affectionate' neither emphasizes or denies it. One could imagine a hug, for instance, being affectionate and yet far from tender."[28]

The role of religion in Winnicott's life was of some importance. He was reared in a nonconformist faith, in which there was an emphasis on deep inner conviction. He seems to have been a religious person in the sense that he maintained a capacity for wonder, and it is the evidence of wonder on the printed page that distinguishes him from so many other psychoanalytic writers. At the same time, he was extremely suspicious of any religion that had the effect of suppressing individual development in favor of compliance with a handed-down program of worship. His attitude toward this could be ferocious. The quality of reverence was paramount. For Winnicott wonder was accompanied by reverence for the objects of wonder. Reverence included but exceeded an

26. To the *Times*, 10 August 1949.
27. To P. D. Scott, 11 May 1950.
28. To V. Smirnoff, 19 November 1958.

attitude of restraint. One did not invade the territory that evoked wonder. One observed and described and acknowledged. And in the same way, one expected to be treated with respect, not preached at or pressured into being something other than what one naturally tended to be.

His family were churchgoers. Clare Winnicott recalls in her memoir that he told the following story: "My father had a simple (religious) faith and once when I asked him a question that could have involved us in a long argument he just said 'Read the Bible and what you find there will be the true answer for you.' So I was left, thank God, to get on with it myself.'"[29] The reasons for or the effects of Winnicott's conversion to Anglicanism in medical school are not known. By 1919 he was saying: "extreme acts and religious rituals and obsessions are an exact counterpart of these mind disorders, and by psychotherapy, many fanatics or extremists in religion can be brought (if treated early) to a real understanding of religion with its use in setting a high ethical standard. Thus they can be brought from being a nuisance to the community and a centre of religious contagion to normal, useful and social members, in a position from which to develop along their own individual lines."[30]

He finds fault with anyone who treats psychoanalytic theory as if it were a religion, or a political view with religious overtones. To Roger Money-Kyrle (23 September 1954): "I think what irritated me was that I faintly detected in your attitude this matter of the party line, a matter to which I am allergic." In a letter to Melanie Klein and Anna Freud (3 June 1954), urging the dissolution of the double training program: "if we in the present try to set up rigid patterns we thereby create iconoclasts or claustrophobics (perhaps I am one of them) who can no more stand the falsity of a rigid system in psychology than they can tolerate it in religion." In the letter of February 1956 to Joan Riviere: "The only thing that can happen is that those of us who like to support Melanie produce, as we could all do, clinical material or quotations from the Bible which support her theme."

29. "D. W. W.: A Reflection," in *Between Reality and Fantasy,* ed. Simon Grolnick (New York and London: Jason Aronson, 1978).
30. To Violet Winnicott, 15 November 1919.

The word "religion" is used most often pejoratively in these letters, but Winnicott also says "One must be able to look at religious beliefs and their place in psychology without being considered to be antagonistic to anyone's personal religion. I have found others who thought I was anti-religious in some of my writings but it has always turned out that what they were annoyed about was that I was not myself religious in their own particular way."[31] It was not religion generally that he opposed, but religion that demanded obedient worshipers. "It is not possible for me to throw away religion just because the people who organize the religions of the world insist on belief in miracles."[32] Religion that quashed creativity, closed systems that did not allow for personal discovery and revision, drew his ire.

When he writes to Melanie Klein that if she will not destroy the language called the Kleinian doctrine "then this artificially integrated phenomenon must be attacked destructively," he is expressing his opposition to a form of idol worship. The perfection of the idol and its corresponding pathological idealization are regarded as deadly. Winnicott's attitude is made clear by his reference to Joan Riviere's portrayal of the Klein theory as an essentially complete theory of human psychology. There is no room in it for individual rediscovery and reformulation, no room for Winnicott himself, nor for anyone else, to contribute.

This point of maximum conflict, the use of aggression to defeat a life-denying theory, must have had roots deeper than a theoretical disagreement with Melanie Klein. Jay R. Greenberg and Stephen A. Mitchell have pointed out that Winnicott misreads Freud's theories as if his own work were a logical development of them.[33] Winnicott takes as basic a relational structure of infant to mother, in contrast to Freud's placement in the same primary position of an instinctual life that is originally without specific objects. As for Klein, Winnicott transforms her theory of the depressive position into what he calls "the phase of concern," and in

---

31. To Michael Fordham, 11 June 1954.
32. To Wilfred Bion, 5 October 1967.
33. Jay R. Greenberg and Stephen A. Mitchell, *Object Relations in Psychoanalytic Theory* (Cambridge, Mass.: Harvard University Press, 1983).

so doing he elevates the mother's actual behavior to an important position. Greenberg and Mitchell discuss Winnicott's ideas in light of a theory of poetic achievement espoused by the literary critic Harold Bloom. According to Bloom the newcomer/son duels with the precursor/father to overcome a sense of belatedness. He can do this only by misreading the work of the precursor, so that the newcomer can have a rightful place in the tradition. This idea lends itself to the study of psychoanalytic theory-making, inasmuch as all who call themselves psychoanalysts purport to continue Freud's work. Klein argued that Freud's notion of a death instinct provided the basis for much of her work. The ego psychologists took another version of Freud as their model. From a technical point of view, some modern-day orthodox analysts practice in an atmosphere that caricatures Freud's technical injunctions in the matter of abstinence and anonymity, while those who apply their rules more loosely always cite the *real* Freud, who sometimes spoke of personal matters, selected a fine cigar to celebrate a fine interpretation, asked certain analysands to translate his papers, or provided food for the hungry Rat Man. There are, of course, all combinations. It cannot be far off the mark to say that each analyst has in his mind a Freud that encompasses crucial aspects of his own personal history.

Freud the great system builder probably meant less to Winnicott than Freud the originator of a method to plumb the human soul. One has the sense that Winnicott did not set his sights on Truth with a capital T, but on truths that would not stay still, the truth that is contained in the continuous interplay of people. He did not seem to require what Nietzsche has called "metaphysical solace," of the sort one may get, for example, from a convincing philosophical system. Yet this feature of his thought constituted a kind of philosophy in itself, as J. P. M. Tizard has pointed out.[34]

In the letters there are numerous references to Winnicott's refusal to use metapsychological terms. For example, to David Rapaport (9 October 1953): "I am one of those people who feel compelled to work in my own way and to express myself in my own

---

34. J. P. M. Tizard, "Donald Winnicott: The President's View of a Past President," *Journal of the Royal Society of Medicine,* April 1981.

language first; by a struggle I sometimes come around to rewording what I am saying to bring it in line with other work, in which case I usually find that my own 'original' ideas were not so original . . ." To Anna Freud (18 March 1954): "I have an irritating way of saying things in my own language instead of learning how to use the terms of psycho-analytic metapsychology. I am trying to find out why it is that I am so deeply suspicious of these terms. Is it because they can give the appearance of a common understanding when such understanding does not exist? Or is it because of something in myself? It can, of course, be both." And to Michael Balint (5 February 1960): "whereas I used to be absolutely unable to take part in a metapsychological discussion, I am now just beginning to be able to see a glimmer of light, so that if I live long enough I feel I might be able to join in from time to time."

It is consistent with his suspicion of metapsychological language that Winnicott seems to have had a reluctance to read Freud. He writes to James Strachey (1 May 1951): "You will be relieved to hear that I have done quite a bit of psychoanalytic reading," and to Ernest Jones (22 July 1952) he speaks of "my inhibitions in regard to the reading of Freud."

Although he often referred to Freud and acknowledged his primacy—"From my point of view any theories that I may have which are original are only valuable as a growth of ordinary Freudian psycho-analytic theory"[35]—Winnicott differs from most major contributors to psychoanalysis in that he maintained a style that was distinctly his own. He rarely tried to translate his ideas into "ordinary psycho-analytic theory." He was set apart, or better, he set himself apart. In a letter to Adam Limentani (27 September 1968), he says "For a long time, as you know, I was not asked to do any teaching of psycho-analysis because neither Miss Freud nor Mrs. Klein would use me or allow their students to come to me for regular teaching even in child analysis . . . When later on I became acceptable and was invited to do some teaching, I had already had some original ideas and naturally these came to mind when I was planning to talk to the students." Having been left out in the cold by the two principal leaders of British psycho-

35. Letter to Harry Guntrip, 20 July 1954.

analysis, he was forced to develop on his own (in the area of technique, at least), and once he started down that path, there could be no turning back. He was compelled, as an original, to remain outside the two inner circles that gave comfort to their membership.

Winnicott's avoidance of the terms of metapsychology, a distinct drawback from one point of view, since so much of what he had to say was not understood and could not be readily integrated into the larger theory, is one aspect of that pattern of self-restraint which permits the liveliness of his thought to flourish and be communicated. Striving to do without received jargon, he was forced to describe what he meant in ordinary language, as clearly as he could. There are few carefully researched reviews of the literature, although he does mention Freud, Klein, and some others. The mood he evokes is light, playful, though not, for all that, unserious. Quite the opposite. His readers get a sense of focus, because they do not have to make their way through very much before coming to the main ideas, which are expressed in everyday language. This appealing clarity may be spurious, because the ideas are not usually as simple as they seem, nor, though original, are they disconnected from the work of others.

As we read his papers and letters, Winnicott drops into our astonished midst like a parachutist who is entitled to be right where he is. He often begins with a few pithy sentences that many another writer would put at the end. His freedom is made immediately apparent. Probably a study of his life would reveal the conditions under which "being himself" had become a continuing issue, but that line of thinking cannot be pursued here. In her memoir, his widow speaks of his childhood as happy, and there is every indication that it was so. There are no spectacularly neurotic parents or major losses. Yet we can detect in these letters the existence of struggle. He gravitated toward a drama in which his special sensitivity to any condition that might thwart his self-expression would be played out. He represented others in his role as sensitive contributor to man's store of knowledge, and he extended his concern to the whole of psychoanalysis. The nearest thing to a direct statement about his struggle is in the important 1952 letter to Klein: "My illness is something which I can deal with in my own way and it is not far away from being the inherent difficulty in regard to human contact with external reality."

By 1952 Winnicott was urging Klein to destroy Kleinianism or face the attacks of others who would have to do it. It is no indictment of the validity of his arguments to imagine that among the sources of his criticism was his earlier intoxication with her ideas. Nor does his argument suffer if we raise the possibility that he underwent a religious struggle of his own (in medical school, perhaps), which sensitized him to the Klein theory as if it were a religion that demanded obedience. His inability or unwillingness to use metapsychological terms may indicate a similar, if less dramatic and flagrant, conflict with respect to Freud.

Reserving for himself the right to search out that fulcrum at which relative significance can be assigned to contending influences, Winnicott shuddered "lest my work should be taken as a weighting on the environmental side on the scales of the argument, although I do hold the view that psycho-analysis can afford now to give full importance to external factors, both good and bad, and especially to the part played by the mother at the very beginning when the infant has not yet separated out the not-me from the me."[36]

In attempting to give proper credit to the role of external events in human development and judgment, Winnicott risked being regarded as one who had lost sight of Freud's revolutionary demonstration that to an extraordinary degree it is the unconscious that orders our perception of the external world. What a psychoanalyst offers a patient is a new view of himself, and an opportunity to make new choices based upon deep knowledge of all relevant factors. Klein had taken Freud's emphasis to unreasonable levels, virtually excluding external reality from causative import in the life of the mind. In correcting her extravagance, Winnicott introduced an array of unique ideas to a wider field of psychological science.

He introduced the concepts he called "primary maternal preoccupation," "good enough mother," "ordinary devoted mother,"

36. To the *Times*, 10 August 1949.

"the phase of concern," "the holding environment," "transitional objects and transitional phenomena," "impingement," "regression to dependence," "true and false self," "squiggle," "the antisocial tendency."[37] He developed a comprehensive theory of normal and pathological infant development. He addressed the subjects of childrearing; play in all its forms; the relating of individual life to group, social, and cultural life; criminality; psychoanalytic technique. He was the first to approach in an analytic fashion a ques-

37. "Primary maternal preoccupation" is mother's state of mind in the weeks before and after childbirth: she is preoccupied with her infant and somewhat withdrawn from other concerns. The terms "good enough mother" and "ordinary devoted mother" reflect Winnicott's belief that almost all mothers are effective, and that they do not have to meet anyone's definition of perfection to be so. "The phase of concern" is Winnicott's term for Klein's "depressive position." The leading characteristic of this phase is the infant's concern with his mother's welfare. Winnicott's definition emphasizes the normal development of morality and removes the pathological overtones of Klein's phrase. The mother as a real person, rather than only a product of the child's fantasy, is central to his viewpoint. "The holding environment" is all nurturing aspects of the child's environment, including actual physical holding. The mother's preoccupation with the infant is a kind of holding. This environment is reproduced by psychoanalytic treatment in which the analyst is concerned with the patient's state of mind, and it becomes especially important when the patient is regressed. The term "transitional objects" refers to particular toys or objects, such as blankets, from which young children become inseparable, and which they use to produce a soothing experience before sleep. Winnicott believed that at first mothers provide such objects at just the moment when they are needed, thus fostering the illusion in the child's mind of having created them. Starting from this early area of pleasure in illusion, human experience expands to include play, creativity, and cultural life in general. These categories of experience all provide a resting place where strict definition of self and others is not only not required, but is a hindrance to fulfillment. They all occur in the area of overlap between what comes from within and what is given from without. For "impingement," see p. xviii. "Regression to dependence": severely disturbed patients return emotionally to a very early state of development, of which one feature is their absolute dependence on a caretaking person. "True and false self" is Winnicott's term for the gradient between an external, compliant aspect of a person and an internal, authentic, and uncompliant aspect. The gradient exists in normal life, but is exaggerated in certain people who live falsely without being seen as doing so by others, or sometimes even by themselves. "Squiggle" is a game played with children in which therapist and patient make alternating strokes on paper; together they make a drawing that yields vital information about the child's state of mind. "The antisocial tendency": a symptom that is often traceable to a sequence of initial good enough mothering followed in the second or third year by environmental failure such as separation from parents.

tion that had not been considered by psychoanalysts before him: what it is that makes life worth living. And throughout his writings there is an effort to grasp the components of man's experience of reality, a subject closely related to the functioning of the true self.

Those who say that Winnicott placed the therapeutic value of the relationship to the analyst above the interpretive process misread and trivialize his far more complex view. His work survives and continues to be fruitfully quoted in papers on technique precisely because his writings, so widely applicable, do not confirm such a classification. He remained steadfast as a reader of the unconscious and a believer that accurate, well-timed interpretations are the chief instrument of change. It was only in the treatment of deeply disturbed patients that he believed a phase of management to be indispensable. Such patients, regressing to the point where they had been failed in infancy, required a holding environment as the corrective from which a resumption of development might proceed. A version of psychoanalysis as professionalized kindness, psychoanalysis reduced to empathy, or to a long process the denouement of which is confirmation that the patient's life was indeed ruined by his parents, was quite foreign to Winnicott. He said "Psychosis is a deficiency disease," but he knew that to arrive at the point of deficiency required a long period of psychoanalytic interpretation.

Winnicott could not be pigeonholed, easily summarized, or forced into extreme statements intended to cover all psychoanalytic eventualities. There was always balance and the play of the unexpected. By focusing attention on the area of overlap between and among people, from the transitional experiences of infancy to the creativity of everyday life to the pleasures inherent in cultural experience, he was able to avoid making neat categories devoid of the flavor of lived experience. He called our attention to the flux in which life develops and is played out, implying always that life is motion. The Teutonic tradition of category-making, which is the background of psychoanalytic theorizing, would seem not to have found good soil in Winnicott's mind. His sense of irony and comedy was too well-rooted for that to happen.

Being on familiar terms with his own omnipotent urges, Winnicott could afford to let the play of his mind extend to its brilliant and unexpected limits. He knew that the making of mistakes was universal, that they could usually be corrected, that it was worthwhile to permit the words "There is no such thing as a baby" to emerge from his lips. He could afford to be astonished by such a statement, and go on to realize that what he meant was that wherever you found a baby, you would also find a mother, and that the two must always be considered as a pair. That was a single example of his daring.

To one correspondent he wrote: "you can imagine how reluctant I am to start up a 'squiggle technique' as a rival of other projection techniques. It would defeat the main object of the exercise if something stereotyped were to emerge like the Rorschach test. Essential is the absolute freedom so that any modification may be accepted if appropriate. Perhaps a distinctive feature is not the use of the drawings so much as the free participation of the analyst acting as psycho-therapist."[38] He sought to protect delicate, transient actions from the crushing weight of formal classification. He wanted to engender in others a taste for experimental action, which was, from his standpoint, inspired thought manifested in the safety of a relationship. He therefore worked toward creating conditions that would foster the willingness of patients, analysts, and ordinary citizens to make their unique contributions, to risk the spontaneous gesture. He celebrated the emergence of the inner world into forms that others may behold. In giving to Freud's concept of free association an expanded and humanized definition, he advanced the psychoanalytic spirit into new frameworks of relevance.

38. To L. Joseph Stone, 18 June 1968.

The Spontaneous Gesture

We no longer believe that truth remains truth when the veils are withdrawn; we have lived too much to believe this.

—Friedrich Nietzsche

1 ⮞ To Violet Winnicott

62 Oxford Terrace
Paddington W2
November 15, 1919

My dear Violet,[1]

Psychotherapy progresses. Do not trouble to read further as (at your invitation) I am going to explain a little about it.

First a few definitions. Therapy means treatment. Psychotherapy means the treatment of disorders of the mind apart from those depending on disease of the brain. The Brain is the mass of grey and white matter which lies hidden in the skull, whereas the mind is that part of a person which stores memories, thinks and wills (if it does will at all). The brain is unlike the mind as a nerve is unlike the impulse that travels down it.

Suggestion is the active principle of almost all medicine; it is that by which a doctor ensures that a medicine will act. It is the influence of a man's personality and way of putting things over the progress of the patient. Everyone knows how effective and necessary suggestion is in affecting a cure. Hypnotism is a method of giving a concentrated dose of suggestion.

Now then we come to Psychoanalysis. This long word denotes a method developed by Freud by which mind disorders can be cured without the aid of Hypnosis, and with a lasting result as opposed to the temporary cure sometimes produced under Hypnosis. Psychoanalysis is superior to hypnosis and must supersede it, but it is only very slow in being taken up by English physicians because it requires hard work and prolonged study (also great sympathy) none of which are needed for Hypnosis. Only yesterday I saw a man suffering from shell shock put under Hypnosis by the man who looks after mental diseases at Bart's. This man could never do Psychoanalysis because it needs patience and sympathy and other properties which he does not possess.

The discharged soldier was helped a little, perhaps, by the Hypnosis, but he will not be cured because Hypnosis only treats one or two of the symptoms: whereas Psychoanalysis cuts right at the root of the matter.

May I explain to you a little about this method which Freud has so cleverly devised for the cure of mind disorders? I am putting this all extremely simply. If there is anything which is not completely simple for anyone to understand I want you to tell me because I am now practising so that one day I shall be able to help introduce the subject to English people so that who runs may read.

The subject is such an enormous one that I must ask you to assume some astoundingly controversial axioms. For instance we will take it for granted that there is a division of the Mind into the conscious and a subconscious, and that in the latter are stored all impressions received since birth (and possibly before). We can have a diagram

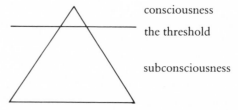

in which a man's mind is represented as a pyramid in subconsciousness with just the tip above the border line. For memory we devise all manner of weird methods for diving into the subconscious. Between one thought and the next there is always some connection or other whether it be a logical connection of ideas, a pun on two words or some other link which turns consciousness into an uninterrupted sequence of events.

I must turn right away now to the instincts. No matter how many there are, but anyhow these are natural directions in which the something which we call the life force must travel outwards.

Again I must go across and state baldly that an idea or an abnormal tendency, so long as it is in the conscious mind or completely understood by the conscious mind, can definitely be controlled by the will in a human being who is not out of mind. But it is equally true that an instinct repressed along abnormal paths is liable to be shoved down deep into the subconscious and there act as a foreign body: this "foreign body" may remain in the subconscious for a whole lifetime and completely control the life of the individual who has no control over this curious tendency since it is not known to him even to exist.

In short Psychoanalysis is a method by which, simply by making one back step after another the patient is led to trace back his dreams and obsessions to their origin which has often been harboured since infancy or childhood. The patient is amazed to find his curious behavior explained and the cause brought up into consciousness. He is then able to bring his own will into the battle and his will is given a fair chance.

Hypnosis you see depends on a patient borrowing will from the physician. Psychoanalysis only gives a man a fair chance to bring his own will against the situation in question. And as a person's will is always sufficient against a realised tendency (as a rough rule) there is great hope for the future.

I shall probably be accused of blasphemy if I say that Christ was a leading psychotherapist. (I don't know why, but Violet is fond of saying that what I say is blasphemy, when there is no connexion whatever between what I have said and the term.) It is no less true that extreme acts and religious rituals and obsessions are an exact counterpart of these mind disorders, and by psychotherapy, many fanatics or extremists in religion can be brought (if treated early) to a real understanding of religion with its use in setting a high ethical standard. Thus they are brought from being a nuisance to the community and a centre of religious contagion to normal, useful and social members, in a position from which to develop along their own individual lines.

So now you know a little about a very vast subject which has the great charm of being really useful. It remains for me to put what I am learning to the test. Even if I do not take up any subject which allows of psychotherapy in my work, the knowledge will always be useful as a hobby.

I have an O.L.[2] called Alcock staying here for the weekend. He is up in order to see his fiancee. He is a friend of the Edes[3] and was a prisoner for a long while in Germany and Holland.

Don't forget the Beethoven to Ona, the tie pin or rather collar pin for myself and *the glasses from Lascelles.*

I hope this letter has not bored you. I have enjoyed trying to say a few facts about my hobby since it is always good to crystallise one's thoughts a little.

> With much love
> Your affec.
> Donald

1. Winnicott wrote this long letter to his sister when he was a medical student. The first few pages have been omitted here.
2. Old Leysian (former pupil of the Leys School).
3. H. S. Ede was Winnicott's best friend at school, and out of this a friendship between the families developed.

2 ▸ *To Mrs. Neville Chamberlain*

November 10th 1938

Dear Mrs. Chamberlain,

I feel the Prime Minister is too busy to answer questions, but I do want to know two things. Would you try to answer this as many of us are urgently in need of answers that we cannot get.

In fact, does the Prime Minister *really* believe that less good management by someone representing the majority vote of citizens is preferable to better management by someone who keeps power by suppression of free thought?

The second is, why does the Prime Minister never mention the Jews. Does he secretly despise them? When in England we say WE, we include Jews who are people like ourselves. I am not asking him to be pro-Jew, but I want to know definitely whether he is or is not secretly anti-Jew . . . at present we seem to be secretly sharing German's anti-Jew insanity, and this is not where we want our leaders to lead us.

> Yours sincerely,

3 ⮑ *To Kate Friedlander*

8th January 1940

Dear Dr. Friedlander:

I was very tired last Thursday evening and partly because of this and partly because your paper suggested several different themes I did not say some things I should have liked to have said on the main point brought forward.

Your observation on the way ordinary people reacted to the war by expressing opinions without being willing to discuss them is certainly valid. I am not quite sure whether you attempted to explain the mechanism of this, but one of your questions was quite simply asking whether others have noted what you have noted. I have.

You would, I suppose, agree there is nothing new in the fact that people hold opinions which they must put forward and which they cannot discuss. You mean that the war became one of these themes that are used compulsively, and that, at the time of greatest stress, people who usually can discuss opinions became temporarily unable or unwilling to do so.

I think it is very interesting to try to find out more about the reason for this change.

The uncertainty must itself contribute largely to the individual's need to employ magic, as Dr. Payne said (following Dr. Kris's introduction to the idea of magic). This leads to the question, why is uncertainty alarming? This in turn leads to the idea of *control*. The greater the uncertainty the greater the need for control, and one method of control is by ideas and statement of words; even evil, when it is predicted is better than the prospect of uncontrolled possibilities.

One would find some individuals who must control in this way, and others who are much less under such a compulsion. A way of classifying these would be to speak of those who need to control (magically) the political situation as those who use the political situation to represent a chunk of their own inner world (or unconscious fantasy) for which they cannot bear full responsibility. This is half way between depression and elation, between carrying the sins of the whole world, and denying responsibility for anything.

In the course of the discussion I said that these people could not brook discussion because they had, in fear of uncertainty and ignorance, made the last possible consultation, they had consulted God. Beyond that is threat of depression or madness, that is, mechanical control or chaos. I put it in this way to introduce the idea that the normal person has "people" inside him, in the fantasy that he *localises* (unconsciously) *inside himself,* and that when anxiety is not great these people are human and open to argument; when anxiety is great, however, their magical qualities increase, and they become Gods.

This method of stating things involves this concept of the *inner world,* the fantasy which is *located,* in the individual's unconscious fantasy, and which is related to intake, retention and excretion experiences. This in my opinion is the part of the psycho-analytic theory which I do not find represented in the Viennese Group's way of looking at things, and I believe this special bit of theory will come up again and again for discussion until we each understand exactly where the other stands.

I cannot say how much I value the discussions in the smaller groups such as Anna Freud's and also my group, where so many points are raised. My regret is that last Thursday I was confused by the number of points you raised, and unable at the time to let you know I appreciated your main point.

Yours very sincerely,

4 ⤖ *To the Editor,* British Medical Journal

22nd December, 1945

Sir,

It is now two years ago that you published two letters from me and many letters from others, on the subject of the new physical methods of treatment of mental disorder, especially electrically induced fits. In these two years a very large number of people have been treated by induced fits; to some harm has been done and some have been "cured." The fact remains, in my opinion, that these forms of therapy have disadvantages, the most serious of which is that false theories of mental disorder are built up round wrong interpretations of the mechanism of these "cures." The medical profession should be reminded from time to time that these treatments are pure "shot-in-the-dark" affairs, and no theory of their action, even when they seem to work, is accepted even by the psychiatrists.

The great example of this bad result of building on other than scientific foundations is provided by the treatment of mind disorder by operation on the brain. In good faith members of our profession are cutting brains about, dividing the associating fibres between the frontal lobes, devising other ways of using their brilliant team work and surgical technique. Yet enough is already known of mental disorder for it to be said that no mentally ill person can ever be made well by operation on a normal brain. In fact, it must be an important part of every leucotomy treatment to see that if the patient gets well enough to go out and do his shopping and go to the cinema he does not also regain the right to vote, or take an active part in the arrangement of our affairs. He is permanently maimed.

I realize that the correct procedure is for us to speed up research into the psychology of insanity and so to provide a scientific basis for mental hospital work, but in the meantime are we to see our countryside littered with "cured" mental hospital patients with permanently deformed brains? And what happens if these physical therapy methods spread to the treatment of criminals? What guarantee have we that a Bunyan in prison will be allowed to keep his brain intact and his imagination free, or, to take a more ordinary case, that a political prisoner should be allowed to maintain his political convictions and his brain.

A new habeas corpus is needed now, a "habeas cerebrum," and very quickly. At any rate I should be grateful if your journal could once again make it possible for it to be said that there is one doctor who thinks the new physical therapy of mental disorder is sociologically dangerous, and that surgical interference with the brain in mental disorders is absolutely never justified.

I am, etc.
D. W. Winnicott.

5 ❧ To Lord Beveridge

15th October, 1946.

Dear Lord Beveridge,

Can you help me out of a difficulty. I am very impressed with the views you hold on our treatment of Germany and for this reason wish to support you strongly. However, as a thinking kind of practising doctor (paediatrician-psychiatrist) I feel that the nationalisation of doctors is destructive of the best in our profession, and one of the chief things that has brought about this is the clause in your famous Report. So from my point of view you are the main cause of a bad thing.

I think your suggestion that the medical profession should be nationalised was made in good faith, and that you were truly ignorant of the harm your suggestion must do. It was true ignorance that allowed you to make medical practice subservient to politics instead of to science, but ignorance cannot absolve you of my hatred.[1]

How can I reconcile my admiration of your new work on behalf of our democratic value, and my hatred of you because of your irresponsible suggestions in respect of doctors?

If you can find time to answer this letter please do not assume that I talk lightly and without true knowledge of medical practice. As a psycho-analyst I have been able to deepen and widen my own considerable experience by intimate knowledge of the feelings of others.

The public cannot of course be expected to understand these things, and very few understand what they stand to lose by the turning of doctors into civil servants; but in your position you cannot be absolved, and I must at any rate be honest with myself and express to you yourself the hate that rises naturally in me, alongside my other feelings for you and your work.

Yours truly,
D. W. Winnicott, F.R.C.P.

---

1. Winnicott's paper "Hate in the Countertransference" was read to the British Psycho-Analytical Society on 5 February 1947. The subject of hate must have been on his mind when this letter was written.

6 ॐ *To the Editor, the* Times

6th November, 1946

Sir,

The National Health Service Bill has been reported in its various stages but for some reason it has scarcely been discussed in your columns; nevertheless it is bound to be far-reaching in its effects. Perhaps, now that it is practically law a letter might be allowed suggesting that a total state medical service can have severe ill-effects.

For instance, one result is that medical practice is now to be subservient not to science but to politics. Whatever gains come from the new scheme these must essentially be out-weighed by the loss of what has been won by the great scientist doctors of our history, and maintained by generations of practitioners in face of continuous public demand for faith-healing and magic.

Already a Minister of Health (without scientific training) has been the one to decide not to include osteopathy and faith-healing in the state medical service. From the doctor's point of view this is exactly as bad as if he had decided the other way. That such decisions should rest with whomever the parliamentary majority happens to give charge of housing, health and a few other odd items, is a depressing thought.

It seems to me to have been the duty and privilege of a paper with the standing of the Times to have put this issue clearly before the public: a body of people, untrained in scientific method but elected because of the complexion of their political views, had finally destroyed a good thing out of ignorance.

I am etc.
D. W. Winnicott

7 ε→ *To Ella Sharpe*

13th November, 1946

Dear Miss Sharpe,

I am very grateful to you indeed for writing about Wednesday's meeting.[1] The subject had to be almost insulted by the fact that I had to speak only for half an hour, when really the original plan in my mind was for six or more discussions.

As a matter of fact, I am not certain that I agree with you about psycho-analysis as an art. Out of your very wide experience there is something that you want to say, and which you express in this way. But from my point of view I enjoy true psycho-analytic work more than the other kinds, and the reason is to some extent bound up with the fact that in psycho-analysis the art is less and the technique based on scientific considerations more. Therefore, when I hear you speak about psycho-analysis as an art I find myself in difficulties; not wishing to completely disagree with you, but fearing lest this comment which you make should be given too much importance. There is obviously plenty of room for discussion here, but I thought I would let you know what I feel, because I usually find [when] I talk on non-analytic aspects of psychiatric work, that [people think] I am making an indirect comment on true analysis which I am not making.

1. Miss Sharpe had written a complimentary letter about Winnicott's paper "Consultation Technique," read 6 November 1946. She had taken part in the discussion.

8 ε→ *To Anna Freud*

47 Queen Anne Street, W. 1.
6th July, 1948.

Dear Miss Freud:

One cannot help thinking about this horrible Mental Health Conference, and your task. As one who was perhaps chiefly responsible for this programme of the Child Section, I feel concerned that one of the aims shall be fulfilled, namely that the work done specifically in Great Britain in the last 25 years, be put forward by whoever is representing Great Britain. For in my opinion, in the natural development of psycho-analysis, it has fallen to the lot of psycho-analysts in this country to bring the aggressive impulses and ideas into their proper place in psycho-analytic theory and practice. Particularly important has been the study of the relation of aggression, guilt and depression, and reparation to each other.

I am rather surprised to find that I owe you a letter on this subject. When I sent you my paper on Aggression (R.S.M.)[1] you wrote and asked me for a summary. It is really awfully difficult to give a summary of so condensed a paper. Either the general tendency and the work it is based on is known and understood, or else (I should say) no summary is of the slightest use. Nevertheless I would say the following:—

(a) In this Congress the important thing to get across is that the world's troubles are not due to man's aggression, but are due to repressed aggression in individual man.

(b) Following this, the remedy is not education of children in ways of managing and controlling their aggression, but is to provide for the maximum number of infants and children such steady and reliable conditions (of emotional environment) that they, each one of them, may come to know and to tolerate as part of themselves the whole of their aggression (primitive greedy love, destructiveness, capacity for hate etc).

(c) To enable human beings, (infants, children or adults) to tolerate and accept their own aggression, respect for guilt and depression is needed, and full recognition of reparative tendencies when they exist.

(d) It is also important to state clearly that in this matter of aggression and its origins in human development there is a great deal that is not yet known.

These themes are developed in my paper.

You will understand that I for one am vitally interested in what you are intending to read in August, and it would give a great relief if you could let those of us who care a lot see what you have prepared in good time, so that discussion of it will be possible.

> With good wishes,
> Yours very sincerely,
> D. W. Winnicott.

1. Royal Society of Medicine.

9 ❧ *To Paul Federn*

3rd January 1949.

Dear Dr. Federn,

I have only just read your lectures on Psychoanalysis of psychoses 1943 and I am writing to say that I have very much enjoyed them. The wealth of clinical experience behind them is so clear. I am very much wanting to have a copy of these for re-reading as the copy I read was a photostat belonging to the U.S. Army. If you happen to have a reprint I would be very grateful if you would send me one. Alternatively I can order a copy of the Psychiatric Quarterly from the publishers. In a week or two I hope to be able to send you a reprint of a lecture of my own on another aspect of the same subject.

You may remember me as the young analyst who never wrote to thank you for taking such a lot of trouble over an article I wrote a long time ago on play or some such subject. That article was written under the influence of Melitta Schmideberg when I was quite unready to write on the theme. The whole thing seemed to me rather unreal at the time and it took me many years to get it into perspective. When you came to England you said to me that this must represent a strong negative transference which had got caught on to yourself. I think this was not correct; there was another explanation, which was that I had been persuaded to do something which was not really part of me and which I really resented.

> With good wishes,
> Yours very sincerely,
> D. W. Winnicott.

10 ❧ *To the Editor,* British Medical Journal

6th January 1949.

Sir:

My friend Dr. Joan Malleson in her letter of December 11th 1948 invites comments from psychologists on the matter of taking the temperature of children by the rectum as advocated by Professor Moncrieff and Dr. Hussey in an article in the previous number.[1]

I hesitated before taking up this matter because my first reaction on reading the article was to feel glad that reference was made in it to the psychological side of the matter. Pediatrics is notoriously out of touch with psychology and here was an exception. Also an infant does not feel much from having a thermometer stuck in the rectum, so that the main trouble comes, if at all, from the interest in his rectum which the nurse must take by using this method. In the majority of cases I imagine there is no special difficulty here except where there has already been a good deal of rectal interference by soapsticks, enemas etc. which has roused resistance in the child to that sort of thing.

As Dr. Malleson has raised the matter, however, I can say that I felt that the words "possible difficulties from the point of view of the psychological trauma . . . are discussed," which occur in the summary of the article, seemed to promise more than actually appeared in the article itself, which really only dealt with what could be called the *human* aspect. We hope this is never missing in the management of children, whether by a physician or nurse.

The trouble is that if a matter like this is to be discussed psychologically, there must be a willingness on the part of all to give time to the discussion and to learn about the use of the techniques by which information can be collected. Even this relatively simple matter of the taking of temperatures by the rectum involves considerations that cannot be put in a letter. Dr. Malleson raises wider issues and it can certainly be said that one cannot do justice to the subject of the effects of enemata for worms and for constipation and other gross anal manipulations except to a group of students who are willing to settle down to a series of 10 or 20 lectures. Even so these lectures would have to be spread over a period of time so that the students could gradually come to be able to get the feeling of the infantile situations, and also in order that they should have opportunity for various kinds of clinical approach to the problems raised in a more theoretical way in the lectures.

It can be said therefore that this subject is not one for treatment in a correspondence column; nevertheless it is only by such means that attention can be drawn to the need for doctors to be willing to treat psychology as a subject comparable to physiology and requiring of the student a hard discipline.

I am, etc.,

D. W. Winnicott, F.R.C.P.

1. The decision to submit this letter for publication was left to Dr. Malleson. She decided against it.

11 *To Marjorie Stone*

14th February 1949.

Dear Mrs. Stone:

Thank you for your letter in which you let me know that you are making dolls to a specification supplied by the Institute of Child Psychology.

I am sure that your motive in making these dolls is a good one, and probably you will be rather surprised to hear that actually I am not at all certain that the idea is sound. At any rate I would like you to know that if there were a public discussion on this matter and I had to take one side or the other, I should probably come down heavily on the side against the distribution of these dolls. You would probably expect a psycho-analyst to hold a different view.

My reasons for this view are more complex than could be stated in a letter. Whilst I appreciate that there are certain children at certain times who might get something out of dolls with sex organs shown, I feel very much more certain that to the vast majority of children it would be exceedingly muddling if they were to find themselves presented with dolls that had these characteristics. I feel that there is much more about a doll than that it is an unalive baby. In fact it is only to quite a small extent necessary that it should look like a baby. It seems to me that the logical conclusion would be to make a teddy bear which really bites if you tease it.

I would of course develop this theme if I felt you were interested, but I thought you would like to know in these few words that I feel that in spite of your good intention you are directing your energies in a direction which is not really desirable.

Yours truly,
D. W. Winnicott, F.R.C.P.

12 ❧ *To the Editor, the* Times

10th August 1949.
Sir,

In your faithful reporting of public affairs you have published several reports, comments and letters in this past week on juvenile delinquency and on the management of Holloway Gaol and on the knotty problem of crime and insanity. It is very seldom that the comments of a psycho-analyst are asked for or printed; instead it is assumed that the psychologist has an attitude, probably a sentimental one. The idea that psycho-analysis has no attitude, but that it can enlighten, seldom percolates.

There is a great danger in the present trend, which some of us predicted. A sentimental swing toward the antisocial child or adult must sooner or later be followed by a reaction. Indeed the sentimentalist in regard to crime is using the criminal for the expression of his own hidden criminality, and is in the same position (but less openly so) as the ordinary man or woman who enjoys crime in the Sunday papers or who reads detective stories. The practice of the Courts must be founded on something more sure than sentimentalism, either on the deep feelings of unsentimental people who can reach to the criminal in themselves, or else on the thinking-out of those who can take into account the unconscious.

There is a very real contribution which psycho-analysis could make, even now, if it were asked to do so. One example could be given right away, and perhaps usefully given. It is this:

Whatever the state of the criminal, old or young, sane or insane, male or female, there is another half of every antisocial act to be considered—society's revenge feelings.

Now public revenge is not necessarily felt in respect of each individual antisocial act, but unpunished misdemeanour or crime swells the reservoir of unconscious public revenge, and unless this revenge is expressed periodically it will come out in some ugly form. The main function of legal procedure is the prevention of lynch-law, which always hangs round the corner even in this country where (because of the success of legal procedure) it is never seen. I have found this view is an extremely unpopular one especially among the sentimentalists in the penal reform movement. The public must be avenged.

What about public education? Cannot the public be educated to see the criminal as an ill person? The answer is that in so far as men and women are conscious of their feelings they can be educated to whatever is truly discovered about the psychology of crime. But people are not like that, and groups of people have always a large central core that is unconscious, and to a large extent unavailable to consciousness even with the help which poets, artists, and philosophers can give those who allow time for that help to operate.

In other words there is a limit to the capacity for each one of us to become fully educated even to what we know to be true. There must therefore always be two points of view. The doctor (psychoanalyst) will surely be more and more liable as time goes on to say: this antisocial child or adult is antisocial because ill. And then the law must follow on by considering how far public (unconscious) feeling needs punishment to be given, regardless of the psychiatric diagnosis.

Only if this simple separation of the two points of view can be made and maintained can the physician of the psyche hope to retain the opportunity to study the antisocial individual as an ill person and to present that point of view when asked!

> I am,
> Yours etc.
> D. W. Winnicott, F.R.C.P.

13 ϡ *To R. S. Hazlehurst*

1st September 1949.

Dear Mr. Hazlehurst:

Thank you for your letter about mine to the Times. I like your classification into two essentials and two accidentals.[1]

It would interest you, I am sure, how in psycho-analytic and also ordinary psycho-therapeutic work, especially with children, the anti-social compulsions come out as symptoms of illness. Especially at their earliest stages it is often quite clear that stealing is an unwelcome thing turning up in the life of the child and bewildering him (or her). Soon, as the child does not understand why he must steal, there comes about a hardening and a whole host of secondary motives, and by that time there is almost no hope of effecting a cure. In the early stages we do seem to bring about a cure in many cases.

Stealing has practically no more relation to poverty and want than civil murder has to persecution.

Yours truly,
D. W. Winnicott

1. The two essentials in punishment were (1) an indication that the law is more than a counsel of perfection and (2) retribution by society. The two accidentals were deterrence and reform.

14 ϡ *To S. H. Hodge*

1st September 1949.

Dear Mr. Hodge:

Thank you for writing to me about my letter printed in the Times. I am interested in what you say,

You will easily understand that in my view the punishment of crime has nothing to do with doing the criminal good. He should really be treated as ill, if the community could allow it, which it can only do to some extent. It could allow it more if there were knowledge and facilities available for *successful* treatments, but it does not interest the public unconscious that criminal symptoms could be treated, i.e. theoretically could be treated.

Your point about the value to the criminal of expiation and propitiation is an immensely interesting one. To some extent the criminal comes in (as a member of society) in his relief at punishment for (even his own) crime. Nevertheless psychology must diverge from the theological view here because the latter have not yet (I feel) been adjusted to the new findings in respect of the unconscious.

We regularly find that at the start of anti-social tendencies in a human being (always in childhood) there is an ordinary strong sense of guilt which (as part of the illness) does not become attached to stealing (or whatever the symptom is) because the individual becomes split. Help given at this point enables the patient to become conscious of a great deal of the conflict and so to reintegrate and to become able to feel guilty about the stealing.

As an example, a child may start stealing because of a feeling of loss of being loved, without knowing at all what is happening. When asked why do you steal, he at first says, truthfully, that he does not know. If the question is repeated he invents reasons rather than feel an ass, or mad, and then (lest the question be asked again) he steals for definite reasons, which he knows. But this third stage is part of a process of hardening. There is no guilt feeling available because the whole thing has become a defensive construction. To reach the guilt one has to get to the individual's original conflict which was there before the stealing started and before he felt a loss of being loved, in fact to that which is common to all human beings: the destructive ideas in the original love impulses. At any stage later than this the individual feels no guilt and in any case his symptom is a reaction to environmental failure—a weakness in the framework life should provide for the developing individual.

I think that in your work you have to take people as they are, apart from their developmental history; also you have to leave out consideration of the repressed unconscious. These two things hamper your work a great deal as in a way you can only deal with the healthy (psychiatrically) personality; yet it is so often the rather unhealthy person who needs help. And it will be many decades before there are enough psycho-therapists competent to help people by freeing their unconscious and with it (in many cases) their guilt feelings and in a more positive sense their sense of concern.

I do hope what I have said may help a little in your understanding of my point of view.

Yours truly,
D. W. Winnicott.

15 ❧ *To Otho W. S. Fitzgerald*

3rd March 1950.

Dear Dr. Fitzgerald:

Thank you for your letter.[1] The real trouble with the psychoanalysts is that they are all working very long hours doing analyses and bearing quite heavy clinical burdens and also teaching those of the people being analysed who are candidates. The strain on the senior members at the present moment is terrific owing to the fact that it takes so long to create an experienced psycho-analyst, and since the war there has been a huge influx of candidates. While deploring this I do personally feel that it has to be accepted because with all the faults, some of them very obvious, which belong to the psycho-analytic society, there is this thing about it— that a consolidated scientific group is building which will be a very important factor in general psychiatric education eventually. What will be most likely to seduce members from these activities at the present time I am not certain. Certainly most of us would feel it to be a waste of time to sit on planning committees arranging some kind of teaching which would be a compromise between what are called various schools of thought.

In my opinion it is the psycho-analytic group which must eventually include what is good in all the other groups, and thinking of the future it is more important that the Society should concern itself with the research which will resolve the disagreements amongst its members than that it should try to be friendly all round. I am afraid that none of the other groups is capable of growing in the same way and eventually including what is valuable in the Freudian group, with the possible exception of the Jungians. In my personal opinion even in this case of the Jungians there is insufficient common ground to enable their society to keep out a lot of psycho-therapists who, while starting off as talented and even brilliant people, have a lack of experience of the psychiatric discipline.

In America I feel the whole thing is quite different, partly because the word psycho-analyst has a much more diffuse meaning, and also because the financial situation is different over there. It is extremely difficult for a senior analyst to earn a good living at present owing to the fact that as a senior analyst most of his patients are candidates, and these are chosen not because of their wealth but because of their suitability.

A further point is that Americans seem to be able to work all day and most of the night although I think this has the drawback of giving them insufficient time to live and think and feel.

At this point in the letter there should come a practical suggestion about the "key which will unlock the barriers between psycho-analysts and organically-minded psychiatrists." I shall want more time before I can say anything about this. What I would do, however, is to make a negative contribution and say that the trouble really is that the unconscious has to be believed in before the psycho-analysts can start talking, and there are comparatively few psychiatrists who can take what has to be said. It is much easier to talk to post-graduate teachers, for instance, or to ordinary medical students, about the unconscious, than to talk to psychiatrists. The fact that I am writing this to you shows that I know there are exceptions. I shall be writing again, I hope.

Yours sincerely,
D. W. Winnicott

1. Dr. Fitzgerald had requested suggestions for bringing together psychiatrists, psychotherapists, and psychoanalysts, as was purportedly being done in the United States.

16 ɞ *To the Editor, the* Times

[probably May 1950]

Sir,

The most important element in our country at any one moment is the ordinary home in which ordinary parents are doing an ordinary good job, starting off infants and children with that basis for mental health which enables them eventually to become part of the community. Nothing must be allowed to interfere with this, which is not only good but also a delicate matter and easily disturbed. It is indeed deplorable that there are homes in which children are neglected or cruelly treated, and organizations such as the National Society for the Prevention of Cruelty to Children which help such children need our support in their difficult task. If, however, by supplementation of those voluntary bodies by some Government department improved access to bad homes should involve the slightest degree of intrusion on the ordinary common good home, more harm than good will be done. Nothing could be more disastrous than the extension of interference by militant sentimentalists who will make parents afraid to be natural.

The danger is that workers with official backing will fear to enter into suspected homes because of the legal safeguards which protect the home from State interference, or else the legal safeguards themselves will have to be diminished and the privacy of the ordinary good home will be lost. Moreover, from the published accounts no one would be able to guess that there is a serious shortage of trained workers so that the implementation of the new Act which has resulted from the valuable Curtis Report cannot be effectual for many years. The cry about children badly treated in their own homes comes from very easily roused pity and not from any knowledge of the actual situation in respect of persons able to do this work well.

I am yours, etc.
D. W. Winnicott.

17 ·❧· *To P. D. Scott*

Dear Dr. Scott:

I think your students are trying to tell you something that I really have said. You will understand that I am extremely keen on penal reform and what I am saying when talking to students is part of the effort towards penal reform. The point that your students refer to is not one that I have made carefully in a published paper although I have often spoken about it.[1] In any case it is very easily misunderstood.

My idea is that any kind of sentimentality is worse than useless. The difficulty is not so much in the feeling that the public has about any one anti-social act. Through identification with the criminal or the anti-social person the public is often extremely sympathetic, and guilty on behalf of the criminal. Nevertheless there is, I am sure, a very real thing which we could call the unconscious revenge reservoir of a community. It would be possible to pass Acts of Parliament which ignore this revenge reservoir. In the extreme of this there would be incidents in which what is called lynch law would come into operation. In fact I would say that the function of judicial procedure is primarily one of preventing lynch law and it does this firstly by taking over responsibility for revenge and secondly by allowing for the cooling of tempers and the operation of objectivity.

I think that it is extremely difficult to get general recognition of this function of judicial procedure, especially amongst the legal profession, who tend to think of the law as a "thing," or at best, an ass, and who fail to see in the judicial procedure expression of their own deep-seated feelings.

Holding these views, I feel that there is a great danger that the reforms which we are trying to bring about will be introduced by cold methods and then swept away by a wave of reaction. The judicial procedure must preserve its function.

Within this framework, I believe that there is room for the advances which psychiatry is beginning to be able to make, although only just beginning. The public in this country is prepared, according to my view, for a certain amount of treatment of anti-social persons instead of punishment. This feeling, I would say, would eventually go into reverse, should it turn out that in actual fact very few criminals can be successfully treated. There is no doubt whatever that even if our knowledge of the psycho-pathology of criminology were to be completed tomorrow, there would still be a very great number of years before psycho-therapists could be properly trained in numbers sufficient to make a practical difference to the problem. But we know that there is so much that we are only just beginning to know, so that in actual fact most of the treatment of the criminal is a matter of research.

The upshot of all this is in my opinion that the psychiatrist's job includes that of reminding the judges and those responsible for judicial procedure that their primary function is to express uncon-scious public revenge in the most civilised way. The psychiatrist is then in a position to give his opinion about a criminal, and it seems to me that we are not far off a state of affairs in which we can say that every criminal is ill. It is for the doctor to say this. It is not for the doctor to say what the public needs in the way of revenge. After judicial procedure has terminated there is room for any amount of research, if the psychiatrists can be used that way, on the treatment of all types of anti-social persons. It seems to me that there are certain types of crime in which our society is ready to treat rather than punish—homosexuality, for instance, and the perversions in general; attempted suicide; infanticide. The appli-cation of all this to anti-social behaviour in children is too big a subject to deal with in a letter.

You will realise I hope that I am a bit of an amateur when I am applying psychoanalysis to this subject, but as you were referring to my views I have tried to explain them.

I am trying to remind myself of having met you or your work but so far without success.

I am enclosing a copy of a letter which I wrote to "The Times" in August last year, and should be grateful if you would return this when you have finished with it.

Yours sincerely,
D. W. Winnicott

---

1. The point referred to is Winnicott's belief that much of the work of penal reform-ers is wasted because the public is, as yet, incapable of accepting it and of giving up the retributive outlook.

18 ☙ *To James Strachey*

1st May 1951

Dear Strachey,[1]

You may have seen from the notices sent round that I am due to give a paper on 30th May on what I am calling "Transition Objects." Actually I am trying to get some of this written out clearly before Whitsun so that it can be circulated. The full paper would be rather a long one.

I am writing to you because I am wondering whether you would agree to read through what I have roughly made of this paper already and let me come and discuss it with you. I am particularly keen to pick up the ordinary psychoanalytic theory in the theoretical section of the paper enough to make what I think is my own contribution acceptable.

You will be relieved to hear that I have done quite a bit of psychoanalytic reading, thanks to having been ill twice; however, it is still true to say that if I were to take a year off and do nothing but read, I would be in a better position for writing papers.

I will be ringing you up about this, but to make a rough suggestion, I would very much like to be able to see you, perhaps Tuesday 8th May any time between 7 P.M. and midnight; if you prefer a morning time, I could probably manage the morning of 8th between 11 and 2. I know that you will tell me if you would rather not burden yourself with this.

Yours very sincerely,
D. W. Winnicott.

1. Strachey had been Winnicott's first analyst.

19 ☙ *To Edward Glover*

23rd October 1951

Dear Glover,

Your letter[1] does not need an answer, but I feel like writing nevertheless as we are colleagues and both human beings.

The point you make gets to the centre of our scientific differences, I think, because you genuinely hold the view that D.W.W.'s ideas (or M.K.'s) are not derived from objective perception of children's ideas, whereas I genuinely believe that they are. At this point I think we can comfortably leave the solution to future observers.

I am sure that your scepticism has a valuable effect, making me a more careful observer, and I expect that my observations have some effect or other on you although I cannot for the moment say exactly what. In any case the review was signed so that everyone is free to feel as you felt when reading the review, that I was talking about "edging away from D.W.W.'s ideas of the child's ideas of the psyche-soma."

> With good wishes,
> Yours,
> D. W. Winnicott.

1. Glover had written to comment on Winnicott's review in the *British Medical Journal* of Melanie Klein's book *The Psycho-Analysis of Children*. After giving initial support to Klein and her theories, Glover allied himself with Klein's daughter, Melitta Schmideberg, who was his analysand, in what amounted to a vendetta against Klein in the British Society. It lasted for years and ended with Glover's resignation.

20 ❧ To Hanna Segal

21st February 1952.

Dear Dr. Segal:

I find I want to say something to you as a result of last night's meeting[1] and I hope you are feeling strong enough; if not, you had better postpone reading this letter until a suitable moment turns up.

. . . I know perfectly well that you are capable of being as humble as anyone else at the right moment, but I think you cannot have any idea how much antagonism you rouse against yourself when you get up at a meeting and say that you are amazed to find that your colleagues (junior of course) have shown that they are capable of doing quite a good piece of analysis and reporting their findings in English which can be understood, etc. etc. I do think that just at times for a few minutes you are tremendously cocksure of yourself, and if you happen to be speaking just then it shows. Perhaps what I am afraid of is that there is terrible disillusionment inherent in all this and I would much rather you knew about it before you come to it. The fact is that you are capable of failing just as other analysts are, because there is so much that we do not yet know. When you talk at these moments of cocksureness you give no indication whatever that you believe that there could be anything that you do not understand.

There are several reasons why I take the trouble to write a letter of this kind. One is because I have a genuine concern for you . . .

With the very greatest pleasure I have watched you develop in analysis and I know of no analysis which has been more success-ful . . .

With all this in mind naturally I am concerned that you shall not spoil it all by getting into some sort of ugly state in which you are sitting perched up on top of a Mount Everest of an internalised good breast.

There is a another reason why I am writing this letter and that is that I am very genuinely concerned with Melanie Klein's contri-bution to psycho-analysis. This contribution of hers is steadily being made unacceptable because of the propaganda indulged in at every meeting, by Dr. Heimann[2] and yourself in particular. There is a saying that good wine needs no bush. In a similar way the good in Melanie's contribution need not be pushed forward at Scientific Meetings. It can be expressed and discussed. At present it is seldom discussed because it is put forward aggressively and then defended in a way which can only be called paranoid. In other words, Dr. Glover's efforts are at last bearing fruit and the Kleinian psychology is organising itself into something which the Klein disciples will preach until it is hated.

Last night I quite enjoyed the three papers. When you got up, however, and showed the fact that these papers were written after the move instead of before, I was immediately taken from my feelings about your statement, and I can assure you that this was the general feeling. The papers could no longer be left to take care of themselves; you had said that they prove something or other and after that the main point was, were you right or not; had they proved some point? In this way the papers suffered and discussion of them was diverted.

Dr. Heimann was nearly as bad in this respect and in any case the way all the sub-Kleinians pop up in defence every time one of them reads a paper gives the impression, which it will take a long time to eradicate, that there is a paranoid organisation amongst the custodians of the good internalised breast.

What is so strange about all this is that Melanie herself is not, as far as I can tell, a bit like this herself. I often feel that she must be very severely hurt by the actions of her friends just as she is hurt by those who refuse to see the value of her contributions. It is notorious that it is more galling to be hurt by one's friends.

You will see that I have let myself go writing to you. My intention is to let myself go in the Society meetings whenever the trend is taken away from scientific statement towards the statement of a political position. I am only waiting for the right moment and probably this would have happened last night if it had not been for Balint, who tried to say something like what I am saying, although he said it in an unfortunate way. I did not want to be associated with him exactly, but I am sure that he is talking about something real.

I sincerely believe that you yourself will want to go into this matter in order to try to see whether what I say is true, which is that Melanie's contributions are being made unacceptable to the Society by the way that about six or eight persons are presenting them in a propagandist way.

> With good wishes,
> Yours,
> D. W. Winnicott.

1. The meeting was a symposium entitled "Reactions of Patients to the New Institutes."
2. Dr. Paula Heimann, one of Melanie Klein's close friends and collaborators.

21 ❧ *To Augusta Bonnard*

3rd April 1952.

Dear Dr. Bonnard:

I wanted to let you know last night that I got on very well with your paper,[1] but at the end you were talking to Gillespie and I had a date with Miss Freud about something.

If there had been a gap I would like to have joined in with congratulations on the analysis itself which is obviously going very well and which you are not hurrying and which you are letting take its own course. This I believe to be the only sensible meaning to the word analysis. I am not by this intending to suggest that one cannot hold up the course of analysis by blind spots in oneself or by ignorance, but I have the impression from your paper that anything that turns up in this case you are able to welcome and to deal with.

If we ever happen to be sitting next to each other over a coffee (or beer!) I would like to discuss with you yet another aspect of the transference situation which I believe you wanted brought out as it is very clearly in your material. This has to do with the way in which you, as one might say, were like a wireless set, only better because human. I mean to say that you were somewhere half between the inanimate object and the total human being. You implied all this, I think, and in this way you as analyst joined up with the fetish objects and the fetish practices which are part of the relationship to objects and yet at the same time in between the actual relationship between whole human beings.

For me this was the most interesting part of the paper although there were many other aspects of your presentation which interested me intensely. I felt I was able to get the idea of what you were like as an analyst from your paper, which is always important when one is thinking of a paper read with the object of the election to membership.

I very much admired the way in which you doggedly went on until the hour was late. This was very sensible of you. I should personally have packed up and regretted it afterwards.

About the telepathy—I have very good evidence in the analysis of a patient to say that one should keep an open mind since patients can become so extremely sensitive to countertransference phenomena, and the appearance of telepathy can easily be given when there is no actual thought transference, don't you think?

With good wishes,
Yours,
D. W. Winnicott.

1. "Polymorph Symptomatology."

22 ᷓ To Willi Hoffer

4th April 1952
My dear Hoffer:

I want to write you about two things.

The first is I want to thank you myself, although I know others have done so, for the very great trouble you took over the Melanie Klein number of the Journal. My regret at not having an article in it is very great, but I have been rather busy re-arranging my private life,[1] which I thought was more important. If the number comes out in book form I hope to have my little bit in it. In any case I feel that the number as it stands is an extremely good birthday present for Melanie, and as I am fond of her as well as deeply appreciating her work I am glad.

I would like also to write a word about what you said at the meeting, partly to agree and partly not. I do agree that Associate Members who are reading membership papers are in a state in which they cannot easily stand criticism. I say that in spite of the fact that I recently wrote a letter which caused a good deal of trouble.[2] If you have heard of this letter I hope you have also heard that I have expressed very deep grief that it was written as it was a thoroughly bad letter. It hurt the reader of the paper but it also hurt me because it obscured the point that I was trying to make which was that I thought the paper was too tidy, not giving away enough of the analyst's way of carrying on.

.   .   .

What I really want to say is this, that there is a great deal to be said for giving the reader of a membership paper every encouragement that can be given. I would not feel, however, that we should sterilise our discussions by feeling unable to use such papers for argument especially as a high proportion of the scientific papers must be membership papers. I well remember my own, which was not a very good one; I remember the discussion became a sort of wrangle between factions which I had no notion of and I just sat back bewildered, quite unable to take part. I cannot remember it having been very traumatic, however. I think I took it as an interesting way into the Society which was evidently not as much in agreement with itself as I had thought.

You may remember some membership papers have been brutally treated. For instance, Rickman's attack on A was quite open; he just said he hated her and the paper and that it was an insult to the Society that the paper was read. I think that there was not much protection of A going on that evening. I remember trying to protect her myself without any success, because I could not think of anything to say.

I would like to suggest that the ability of a reader of a membership paper to stand getting involved in the disagreements in the Society should be one of the many tests of maturity which we require of an Associate Member when electing to membership. I would personally say that the absence of a direct attack on B when he read a really irritating paper was just as harmful to the internal politics of the Society as the open criticism which you felt was made on Bonnard by Melanie Klein when she said that there were things that are already well known which could have been used to do with persecutory anxiety etc. etc.

Before I finish this rather long letter I want to make quite sure that you understand I am trying to write something within the framework of friendship. I have to be on my guard just at the moment because apparently in writing letters I can so easily seem to be quite different from what I feel.

Every good wish and I hope that you and Mrs. Hoffer have a bit of a holiday at Easter, with good weather.

Yours,
D. W. Winnicott.

1. Winnicott had just moved into a new home and office at 87 Chester Square.
2. The letter had criticized the presenter of a membership paper (a paper given as part of the process of applying for full membership in the British Psycho-Analytical Society).

23 ❦ *To H. Ezriel*

My dear Ezriel: 20th June 1952.

I am rather anxious that the matter of your paper[1] should not be left just where it is. From the way you spoke after the meeting I feel that you undoubtedly got a feeling of hostility and I think that the value of the experience of the paper would be lost for you if you were to let this become the main result. The point is that out of an enormous amount of sincere and hard work and original thinking you have presented a paper which is highly condensed and simplified and practically no-one understood what was happening. I think it can be assumed that this is to some extent our own difficulty in coming to grips with your language; I am not of course referring to the English, which is entirely clear, but to the medium of communication.

It will take me quite a long time to get as far as being able to discuss this paper with you in your own terms. Probably I shall try to get there and I am sure that it would be valuable if I can do so.

I would like to say something at the present time, however, which is my opinion about the difficulty that everyone felt last Wednesday. I think that probably there is something which the speakers, and those who could not speak although they would have liked to have done so, sensed but yet could not come to grips with, and this would probably turn out to be a real psychoanalytic difference of approach. I would suggest that the trouble is that the difference cannot yet be clearly stated by psycho-analysts because they have not yet as a body formulated the platform from which they can talk.

I would personally say that without explicitly stating the fact the psycho-analyst assumes that the beginning of the personality is unintegration[2] and that without the unintegration beginning there is no resting place. (I hope you will understand that I am not referring to secondary chaotic states). You with your affection for gestalt psychology seem to me to be taking the pattern-making as a primary state, whereas for the psycho-analyst the pattern-making is a secondary phenomenon related to primary unintegration. On the assumption of a primary unintegration the individual can enjoy pattern-making but pattern-making which contains a denial of primary unintegration can only lead to obsessional intellectualization and to a theory-building which cannot be discussed except by others who happen to be involved in the same process of flight-from-unintegration pattern-seeking.

You will see perhaps from this that I do believe that there is a very deep-rooted difference between your approach and the psycho-analytic and that it cannot be openly discussed because no-one can come to grips with the psycho-analytic evaluation of the unintegrated state and also because you are unable to show quite openly what I believe is implicit in your work which is that to some extent pattern-making is taken by you as a primary function and carries with it some denial of the fundamental value of primary unintegration.

The only satisfactory way out of primary unintegration is the individual's experiences of the instinctual field; pattern-making must always be subservient to this in health. For this reason when people discuss your version of pattern-making and your statement that fantasies deal in some way or other with other fantasies, they will always do as I think Dr. Heimann did on Wednesday, namely ask you "What about dynamics and what about impulses?" and the discussion can never resolve because neither the questioner nor yourself know what is going on. And there is nothing to be ashamed of when there is something which is not yet understood. The danger is that when two people who know they do not agree begin arguing they get into an interminable discussion and each gets the feeling that the other is in a hostile mood.

Whether what I have written makes sense or not, I hope you will take it as an indication of friendliness and of a very deep desire that ultimately your work may join up with the general body of psycho-analytic work, which I believe it does not yet do. I am sure that that is what you really want.

Yours,
D. W. Winnicott.

1. A membership paper.
2. See letter to Masud Khan, 26 June 1961.

24 ⊱ To Ernest Jones

Dear Ernest Jones:

22nd July 1952.

I was very grateful to you for reading and commenting on my lecture "What is Psycho-Analysis?"[1] It is strange how a stupid thing like "not very voluminous" creeps in. It might interest you to know the explanation of this. In 10 years' analysis Strachey made practically no mistakes and he adhered to a classical technique in a cold-blooded way for which I have always been grateful. He did, however, say two or three things that were not interpretations at a time when interpretation was needed. Each one of these has bothered me and at some time or other have come out in an unexpected way. One day, instead of making the interpretation which I can now easily see for myself, about my inhibitions in regard to the reading of Freud, he took up the attitude of trying to persuade me to make the effort and he used the words "after all the part that you need to read is not very voluminous." I am very angry indeed that I have allowed this to come in and I am getting these words crossed out in all the copies that I am sending round.

I am not so ashamed about saying that Shakespeare knew as much as a psycho-analyst as although I agree that the word "knew" is wrong at any rate it is a point of interest for discussion and not a mistake like the other.

With very good wishes,
Yours,
D. W. Winnicott.

1. This paper was originally given in 1945 to the top form of St. Paul's School, London. It was published under the title "Towards an Objective Study of Human Nature," in *The Child and the Outside World* (London: Tavistock, 1957).

25 ⊱ To Melanie Klein

Dear Melanie:

17th November 1952.

I want to write to you about last Friday evening's meeting,[1] in order to try to turn it into something constructive.

The first thing I want to say is that I can see how annoying it is that when something develops in me out of my own growth and out of my analytic experience I want to put it in my own language. This is annoying because I suppose everyone wants to do the same thing, and in a scientific society one of our aims is to find a common language. This language must, however, be kept alive as there is nothing worse than a dead language.

I said that what I am doing is annoying, but I do also think that it has its good side. Firstly, there are not very many creative people in the Society having ideas that are personal and original. I think that anyone who has ideas is really welcome and I always do feel in the Society that I am tolerated because I have ideas even although my method is an annoying one.

Secondly, I feel that corresponding to my wish to say things my way there is something from your end, namely a need to have everything that is new restated in your own terms.

What I was wanting on Friday undoubtedly was that there should be some move from your direction towards the gesture that I make in this paper. It is a creative gesture and I cannot make any relationship through this gesture except if someone come to meet it. I think that I was wanting something which I have no right to expect from your group, and it is really of the nature of a therapeutic act, something which I could not get in either of my two long analyses, although I got so much else. There is no doubt that my criticism of Mrs. Riviere was not only a straightforward criticism based on objective observation but also it was coloured by the fact that it was just exactly here that her analysis failed with me.

I personally think that it is very important that your work should be restated by people discovering in their own way and presenting what they discover in their own language. It is only in this way that the language will be kept alive. If you make the stipulation that in future only your language shall be used for the statement of other people's discoveries then the language becomes a dead language, as it has already become in the Society. You would be surprised at the sighs and groans that accompany every restatement of the internal object cliches by what I am going to call Kleinians. Your own statements are of course in quite a different category as the work is your own personal work and everyone is pleased that you have your own way of stating it. The worst example, perhaps, was C's paper in which he simply bandied about a lot of that which has now come to be known as Kleinian stuff without giving any impression of having an appreciation of the processes personal to the patient. One felt that if he were growing a daffodil he would think that he was making the daffodil out of a bulb instead of enabling the bulb to develop into a daffodil by good enough nurture.

You will see that I am concerned with something which I consider to be much more important than this paper of mine. I am concerned with this set-up which might be called Kleinian which I believe to be the real danger to the diffusion of your work. Your ideas will only live in so far as they are rediscovered and reformulated by original people in the psycho-analytic movement and outside it. It is of course necessary for you to have a group in which you can feel at home. Every original worker requires a co-terie in which there can be a resting place from controversy and in which one can feel cosy. The danger is, however, that the coterie develops a system based on the defence of the position gained by the original worker, in this case yourself. Freud, I believe, saw the danger of this. You are the only one who can destroy this language called the Kleinian doctrine and Kleinism and all that with a constructive aim. If you do not destroy it then this artificially integrated phenomenon must be attacked destructively. It invites attack, and as I tried to point out, Mrs. Riviere's unfortunate sentence[2] in her otherwise excellent introduction puts the matter exactly into words which can be quoted by people who are not necessarily the enemies of your ideas but who are the enemies of systems. Mrs. Riviere's sentence, which I believe you yourself dislike, gives the impression that there is a jigsaw of which all the pieces exist; further work will only consist in the fitting together of the pieces.

The fact is that further understanding such as you have been able to bring through your work does not bring us towards a narrowing of the field of investigation; as you know, any advance in scientific work achieves an arrival at a new platform from which a wider range of the unknown can be sensed. Your work has made us see that the insanities will one day be understood mainly in psychological terms. It is no disgrace that psycho-analysis even represented by its chief exponent, which is yourself, cannot give a clear statement as to why a child is a bed-wetter or why we smoke; that the psychology of delinquency has not yet been tackled in the Society because the main clues are missing; and that you carefully choose patients for teaching purposes and also for therapeutic work.

Those who know your work extremely well nevertheless have their failures, including suicides.

Further I would say that a book like that of Adrian Stokes[3] shows that it is not yet safe to do the analysis of a poet. The psychology of artistic creation and therefore of the creativity that infuses life in general is not covered even if one studies all the work of yourself and those who help to explain your work. All this is a great stimulus and anyone who has an original idea is welcome and I believe we will always be able to tolerate an initial statement in personal terms. The initial statement is usually made at great cost and for some time afterwards the man or woman who has done this work is in a sensitive state as he is personally involved.

In recent weeks a paper of Rowley,[4] with his use of the word collusion, contains original work which can be withered by the sort of treatment that Dr. Heimann gave it. Fortunately there are others who can see that he is a sincere and creative person who is at present speaking his own language, nevertheless using words that we can come to understand.

There is one more point, and that is that I feel that you are so well surrounded by those who are fond of you and who value your work and who try to put it into practice that you are liable to get out of touch with others who are doing good work but who do not happen to have come under your influence. I would have mentioned this on the evening that we were there in your house with the Stracheys if it had not been for the fact that Eric and Judy[5] were present. When you took it for granted that it is impossible that D could do a good analysis of E I felt that you were making a great mistake. Mr. Strachey is too polite and in any case too lazy to take up the matter with you but of course he knows that D is capable of doing a good analysis and so do I. It is true that wrong things will be done and that a great deal will be left out that could be done; nevertheless an opportunity will be given to this man to be creative in a regular setting and he will be able to grow in a way that he was not able to grow without analysis. I think that some of the patients that go to "Kleinian enthusiasts" for analysis are not really allowed to grow or to create in the analysis and I am not basing this on loose fantasy but I am seriously bringing it forward as a matter for thought. I believe that the idea expressed in my paper, however badly it is done, is in the direction of giving a new emphasis so that those who use your concepts and your ideas and your technique may not forget something which it is disastrous to leave out.

I do know that in your own analyses nothing of this that I am criticising occurs. I have no difficulty whatever in telling anyone who asks me, from the bottom of my heart, that you are the best analyst as well as the most creative in the analytic movement. What you do not meet, however, is the opposition to Kleinism which I used to think was simply an invention of [Edward] Glover's but which I now have to admit exists as something which is as much a barrier to the growth of scientific thought in the Society as Darwinism was to the growth in biology so greatly stimulated by the work of Darwin himself. I suppose this is a phenomenon which recurs and may be expected to recur whenever there is a really big original thinker; there arises an "ism" which becomes a nuisance.

I am writing all this down to show why it is that I have a real difficulty in writing a chapter for your book although I want to do so so very badly. This matter which I am discussing touches the very root of my own personal difficulty so that what you see can always be dismissed as Winnicott's illness, but if you dismiss it in this way you may miss something which is in the end a positive contribution. My illness is something which I can deal with in my own way and it is not far away from being the inherent difficulty in regard to human contact with external reality.

Yours,

D. W. Winnicott.

1. Winnicott had read "Anxiety Associated with Insecurity."
2. The unfortunate sentence, which appeared in Riviere's Preface to Melanie Klein et al., *Developments in Psycho-Analysis* (London: Hogarth Press, 1952), reads as follows: "[Klein] has in fact produced something new in psychoanalysis: namely, an

integrated theory which, though still in outline, nevertheless takes account of all psychical manifestations, normal and abnormal, from birth to death, and leaves no unbridgeable gulfs and no phenomena outstanding without intelligible relation to the rest."

3. *Smooth and Rough* (1951), in *The Critical Writings of Adrian Stokes,* II (London: Thames and Hudson, 1978).

4. J. L. Rowley, a member of the British Society.

5. Klein's son and daughter-in-law.

26 ᭙ *To Roger Money-Kyrle*

27th November 1952.

Dear Money-Kyrle:

It was very good of you not only to come to the meeting at Melanie's but also to write to me. I have read what you have written a few times and I am beginning to understand your way of putting things.

Perhaps I could start off with your last paragraph, in which you do find a definite overlap of your views and mine and Mrs. Milner's. I am often thought to be talking about mothers, actual people with babies, as if they were perfect or as if they were corresponding to "the good mother" which is part of the Kleinian jargon. Actually I always talk about "the good-enough mother" or "the not good-enough mother" because in point of fact we are talking about the actual woman, we know that the best she can do is to be good enough, and the word "enough" gradually (in favourable circumstances) widens in scope according to the infant's growing ability to deal with failure by understanding, toleration of frustration, etc. "The good mother" and "the bad mother" of the Kleinian jargon are internal objects and are nothing to do with real women. The best a real woman can do with an infant is to be sensitively good *enough* at the beginning so that illusion is made possible to the infant *at the start* that this good-enough mother is "the good breast." Similarly in analysis the analyst must always be failing; but if one is to get the full blast of the disillusionment or the hate one must first of all make contact by active and sensitive adaptation so as to become good enough, otherwise nothing happens. Rowley might say we must collude with the patient; other people like Miss Freud might point out the need for going slowly so that the processes get established and so that we may *go along with* these processes, without jerky goodness or badness. Following the innate processes in the patient is our way in analysis of making active sensitive adaptation, just as the mother does (if she is good enough) when she cares for the infant to whose care she is devoting herself. At this very early level of working there is no failure except environmental failure, and if one reaches this sort of work in analytic work one has to deal with one's own failure which recurs and which strangely enough tends to take on the pattern with each patient of the environmental failure of that patient. In other words, when we fail with our patient we can look into our own unconscious countertransference or our own inhibitions or compulsions and be as self-critical as we like, but with the patient we must be able to see the failure as something that the patient has enabled us to do in a particular way so as to bring the original environmental failure into the present moment. It is by this process that the work is done although in order for this work to be done there has to be a close adaptation to the patient's needs, in other words an imitation of the good-enough mother who has to start off with extreme sensitivity to the infant's needs. I hope this will be acceptable to you as an enlargement of your last paragraph.

It is only by this means that we come to understand the environmental factor. It is true that the personal factor is what comes up for analysis and unless there is work being done at a very early level the failure is always personal to the patient. At the earliest level, however, and the level to which we must be able to get, the failure is a failure of the analyst, unless it be a deficiency based on physical brain defect.

I get cross when people talk of the "good" or the "bad" mother (breast) when describing actual people (feeding), but I also get cross when the mother is described as "idealised." This again is a term which can be applied to patients from the child's fantasy system and there is the denigrated or shadow (Jungian) mother equally important. The latter is also not a description of a woman. This idea of idealised cannot be applied to the infant at the begin-

ning who is not organised enough to deal with the difference between fantasy (in which idealisation can be represented) and fact.

Now about your four mothers:—

First, the perfect mother from the child's point of view is a
good-enough mother who is adapting well enough at the beginning and who gradually fails to adapt according to the changes
occurring in herself and according to the growing infant's ability
to account for failure. I cannot follow your own description here
about a perfect mother because I think you make this mistake of
not distinguishing between the two tasks of describing ideas and
the actual person of the mother. You do nevertheless separate out
ideas and sensation and I find this useful although there probably
are other ways of expressing oneself in this field. I think I would
rather say the difference between ideas and experience. There is a
very interesting question raised here, however, about the origin of
aggressive impulses. In my opinion the aggressive impulse that is
inherent is extremely powerful and is part of the instinct which
calls out for relationships. It is therefore an essential part of the
primitive love impulse. There is a lot that could be said here about
the pathology of the variable amount of aggression that can be
unavailable for fusion with the love impulse on account of its
being roused before the Ego has developed to the point of being
able to survive the infant's experience of hunger. But this is by the
way. I am sorry that you bring in the death instinct here because
it muddles everything up, and from my point of view it is a concept which Freud introduced because he had no notion whatever
about the primitive love impulse. In an argument it would never
be of the slightest use to bring in the word death instinct unless
you go right back to Freud and talk about the tendency of organic
tissues to return to the inorganic state, which as far as psychology
is concerned means nothing at all except a statement of the obvious. It is probably not even true even in its most crude and
simple form.

You next come to the good-enough mother, which is from my
point of view an ordinary mother who is fond of her child. You
leave out a great deal including the amazing ability of the ordinary
uneducated mother gradually to lessen adaptation according to the
infant's growing ability to deal with failure, for instance by intellectual understanding.

Your next in the category is the ordinary mother, who in my opinion is the same as the other two. You ascribe to her, however, because of her occasional frustrations, the origin of the persecutory and depressive positions, which is something quite contrary to what I believe to be in Mrs. Klein's work and certainly untrue. The depressive position is something absolutely inherent in the growth of the human infant except that it appears only when development of the individual infant is going well and integration has been achieved and a person in the environment is providing a continuous relationship. As for the persecutory position, this requires a great deal more working out and we ought not to lean back on it for the present until we know more about the variable aggression reactive to impingement and its relation to the inherent aggression that is part of the primitive love impulse. You bring in the words "persecutory and depressive positions" in a way that makes me think that just for the moment you are using a cliche and I got the same impression when you spoke about the death instinct.

Your fourth mother is a bad mother. This time you are talking about an actual mother. Can you really only think of badness in quantity of frustration? When we come to a description of a bad mother I think we can have a more interesting view. This is the bad mother, for instance, who tantalizes by being alternately adaptive and non-adaptive as for instance when she is liable to be preoccupied, now with the infant, now with something else. A bad mother is also one who is in pieces, that is to say when several people are looking after an infant, so that the infant experiences a complexity instead of a simplicity in the infant's physical care. Really one could say that a bad mother is the name we give not to a person but to the absence of someone who is just ordinarily fond of the infant. You say with a bad mother persecutory anxiety is very severe, but surely this is assuming that the infant gets as far as being able to feel the return of projected hate. There is a long road before this and if the mother is not good enough the infant fails to integrate or fails to lay the foundation for experiences in relation to what we, looking on, would call the world external to the infant.

From my point of view there is a very simple statement of the infant's relation to the external world. Either the world impinges on the infant; if this is the pattern the infant reacts and in order to regain a personal sense of entity has to withdraw: on the other hand if the pattern is that the infant discovers the world by impulse, movement, gesture, salivation, sight, etc., then the contact with external reality has in itself been part of the life of the individual and we can leave out that which I describe as a withdrawal from contact for the re-establishment of the sense of being. In this paragraph you once again bring in the life and death instincts; you say if they are part of our innate endowment a wholly bad world would be no more possible than a perfect one. This is an example of the way in which the concept of the life and death instincts bypasses the very rich field of enquiry which belongs to early infantile development. It is a pity that Melanie has made such a big effort to bring her view round to a friendship with the life and death instincts, which are perhaps Freud's one blunder. I need not remind you that he was very doubtful about them when he first introduced the concept; also that the term death instinct is abused in our Society more than any other term and used instead of the word aggression or destructive urge or hate in a way that would have horrified Freud, I am sure.

Going back a little further in your letter to your second paragraph, I hope that you will keep an open mind about this business that sensation is that which frustrates and ideas apparently do not frustrate. I believe that this is a very wonky idea. Conflict can occur very early in the infant who cannot go forward in emotional development because of being unable to ride the instincts[,] and backward development means loss of sense of being. Frustration of instinct in the physical sphere is only a little part of all this, and as you know inhibitions are powerful so early that they are often much more the dominating thing than frustration. It seems to me that in the last part of this paragraph you make a noble attempt to state the intermediate area to which I am trying to draw attention. You will remember that the word intermediate was handed to me by yourself during the discussion of the paper on transitional objects and phenomena. The word intermediate is certainly useful but the word transition implies movement and I must not lose sight of it otherwise we shall find some sort of static phenomenon being given an association with my name. This reminds me that in a paragraph of the version of the paper that I handed round before the Friday discussion I said that as well as the capacity for interpersonal relationships and of the fantasy elaboration of this and as well as the personal inner world of psychic reality there is a third equally important thing, which is experience. Experience is a constant trafficking in illusion, a repeated reaching to the interplay between creativity and that which the world has to offer. Experience is an achievement of ego maturity to which the environment supplies an essential ingredient. It is not by any means always achieved. Fairbairn is right here when he points out that the sense of futility, by which I mean inability to feel experiences as real, dominates the symptomatology of the average analytic patient especially when one has begun to go deep.

I think we must take it for granted that emotionally there is no contribution from the individual to the environment or from the environment to the individual. The individual only communicates with a self-created world and the people in the environment only communicate with the individual in so far as they can create him or her. Nevertheless in health there is the illusion of contact and it is this which provides the high spots of human life and which makes the arts among the most important parts of human experience.

Yours sincerely,
D. W. Winnicott

27 ⪦ *To Herbert Rosenfeld*

22nd January 1953.

Dear Dr. Rosenfeld:

I feel like writing a letter about last night's meeting[1] for you to read at your leisure as there is nothing important or urgent in it.

Firstly, I think that the idea of discussing published papers is a good one. I am glad you have set the fashion. The meeting, however, seemed to me to be a dull one and I suppose the reason lies with all of us, myself included.

I have tried to think out what was the matter and I think that one reason is that we did not know what we were discussing. Were we discussing your main thesis, which is, as I understand it, that psycho-analysis can be applied to psychotics, that is to say, work by use of the transference neurosis or psychosis. Or were we discussing the understanding of schizophrenia?

I found, talking to people afterwards, that no-one knew the subject of the discussion and that there was a general bewilderment. Perhaps you will agree with this and it is very easy to look back afterwards.

In regard to the first point, I feel that your two papers have a great deal of merit, but there is of course not much point in getting up and saying this.

In regard to the second point, I tried to say that I fully support the idea that psycho-analysis of psychotics can be done. This thesis still needs working out, however, and I do not consider that you have got very far with working it out, especially in view of the fact that you slur over the management problems. I know of one analyst who knew your patient and who said that the whole work of the management was a very specialised business and that as far as could be seen the bit of work which you did by analysis made no appreciable difference to the patient. I can well believe this to be true. If you would acknowledge it I would support your idea that the work you did is valid as a research and interesting enough to report.

In regard to the third point, I find myself in quite violent disagreement with the general tendency of your paper. I think that the work of Melanie Klein leads up to the beginning of the understanding of these psychotic people. It makes us realise how very much at the beginning of the whole thing we are. There is so much in a psychosis which cannot be explained along the Kleinian lines that the future of analytic research becomes an exciting thing. The implication that the Klein statements really can be extended backwards to cover the very primitive infantile problems is likely to do Mrs. Klein's work very great harm and I think that those who support her should make an effort to be dogmatic only where her work actually applies. I hope you will not react to this as if I am making an attack on Mrs. Klein. I really am extremely concerned with the way in which her position as a pioneer is being undermined by her followers at the present time. You who know her work so well should be helping her to see that the work has its natural limitations. I would very much like to have more chance to talk on this subject with the grouping of those analysts who are particularly associated with Mrs. Klein's work, her supporters as one might say. I am really alarmed by the harm that is being done at the present time by her supporters. The dullness of yesterday's meeting is the result of the years of propaganda by which these supporters have battered down the gestures of those who feel, indeed know, that there are other things in human nature than those tremendously important mechanisms which Melanie Klein has shown us how to see and use.

I tried very hard to get you to allow yourself to bring in the importance of the mother's behaviour at the very beginning but you got away from this as quickly as possible. If it is possible for an analyst or for a mental hospital to cure a schizophrenic patient it must certainly be possible for a mother to do so while the infant is right at the very beginning, and the logical conclusion is that the mother often prevents schizophrenia by ordinary good management. You spoke about the distress of the mother whose baby is already paranoid, and I well know this to be true. What you left out is the fact that a high proportion of infants of the world are seen through infancy by their mothers in such a way that they do not have to have subsequently the therapeutic care of the mental hospital or the psycho-analyst. I was hoping that you would find it possible just to mention the role of the mother in her adaptation to the needs of the infant who is not disturbed; otherwise you are implying that there is nothing but a technique which the infant requires, and this would be an adoption of the worst bit of Anna Freud's way of talking without allowing for all the things that she says about infant care which show that she really knows that there is more in it than a series of techniques.

I am also very worried when people like yourself take back the origin of the sense of guilt too early, thereby failing to give the impression that you understand the fact that it is a very great achievement in the development of the human infant when guilt is experienced. Melanie Klein's most important contribution from my point of view is her theory of the gradual build-up of the capacity to feel guilt, and if somebody says that this is almost a quality of the newborn infant, as you seemed to do last night, then in my opinion what is being shown is that Mrs. Klein's work on the depressive position is not fundamentally understood. You would no doubt be able to show me where I have misunderstood you if we had opportunity for conversation.

I am not able to forget, and I am sure you would not wish me to forget, that those who follow Mrs. Klein have their failures just the same as other people do. Melanie herself has turned down one or two students as unanalysable, a very brave thing to do. You yourself have recently had a failure . . . You felt that you understood him although I myself felt that you were wrong in what you interpreted to me. This would not have mattered, however, had you been able to manage the external situation . . . [Y]ou have nothing to be ashamed of in the fact that you failed. Nevertheless failure has to be acknowledged. I believe that you could contribute in a very important way if you could give a paper on F to the Society, so that the discussion could range around the reasons for failure.

In regard to the patient that you reported, I believe that the treatment ceased, did it not, because the parents came home? This is the sort of thing that requires management. You did not have time to tell us what you did in regard to the man's mother so that we could not discuss whether someone else would have been able to have dealt with that factor, which is a part of the man's illness, a bit of the early management followed through to the present day.

I will not burden you with further comments but I am writing these and sending them to you because I believe that you would like me to do so. I do value your work and I understand that G has asked you, quite off her own bat, if you would discuss a psychotic child patient with her one day. If she perseveres with this request I very much hope you will agree as she has exceptional experience with children, but inherently in her nature a very great difficulty in joining up what she is able to do with theory. She seems to be recovering gradually from this personal difficulty.

Every good wish,
Yours sincerely,
D. W. Winnicott.

1. Dr. Rosenfeld had opened a discussion on his two recently published papers on schizophrenia.

28 ❧ *To Hanna Segal*

22nd January 1953.

Dear Dr. Segal:

I am writing assuming you would welcome a further discussion of the point you made at the meeting last night. You seemed to say that of course every analyst knows that the patient has management needs. You mentioned the fact that no-one would analyse somebody who had not had food for five days. Presumably they would give food. You went on to imply that there is no essential difference between the management needs of a psychotic and a neurotic patient. If you really mean this, heaven help your psychotic patients, and until you recover from this point of view I am afraid you will not make a very interesting contribution to the theory of psychosis.

If you really believe, as many of us do, that the psychotic patient is in an infantile state in the transference situation, then what you are really saying is that there is no essential difference between the management needs of an infant and those of a grownup. Yet in conversation I am sure that you would admit that whereas a mature person can take part in his own management a child can only take part to some extent and an infant at the beginning is absolutely dependent on an environment which can either choose to adapt to the infant's needs or to fail to adapt and to ignore those needs.

I would say that the management problems are essentially different according to the level of development. If this is so, then management problems must be different in the analysis of psychotics and neurotics. As you know, I am one of those who go a little bit further and who say that in the analysis of psychotics we must actually study what we do when we take part, as we always must do, in management. It is not necessary for you to agree with this but your extreme view that you expressed last night seems to me to be one that you might easily wish to correct on another occasion.

One day when we meet we will be able to discuss this. Meanwhile, every good wish,

Yours sincerely,
D. W. Winnicott

29 ❧ *To W. Clifford M. Scott*

19th March 1953

My dear Scott:

The discussion last night[1] did not cheer up until the very end and then I was unable to go over the ground to my satisfaction. Thank you for your contribution, which as usual was full of interest. I think I can recapture some of your remarks.

I feel that there is this essential difference between the criminal and the lunatic; the criminal is not so ill in that at the moment of crime he has hope of an escape from madness or lack of contact or aphanasis etc., and he or she forces the community to meet the symptom. The contact between the criminal and society is very much part of the antisocial's illness. The lunatic, on the other hand, is ill and either gets cared for because of being a nuisance or because of society's distress or society's irritation at parasitism which lunacy brings with it.

In my opinion the difference between prisons and asylums, which may in fact, be very similar, can only be satisfactorily described in terms of this difference between the criminal's relation to society and that of the lunatic. In terms of childhood illness this means that the antisocial child, often a hopeless case, always gets attention, whereas the mad child finds it very difficult to get proper attention. Indeed madness is not recognised in childhood by society and treatment for the mad child is often lacking unless the child can turn round into being antisocial. Do you agree with this sort of statement?

Another comment you made was related to the difference between the first and the subsequent interviews. I think you realise that it was deliberate on my part, as it always is, in these cases, that I did everything I damned well could in the first interview, much more than I would do in any psycho-analytic interview, and then I deliberately did less and less. By the time the child had looked at me and had begun talking to me instead of communicating with me as with an internalised figure, I quickly became human, which means only very ordinarily understanding. He in a corresponding way gave me less and less clues. Eventually he was simply playing and I was a grownup watching and providing toys.

I believe that you thoroughly agree with this, which is in a way the only alternative to carrying the case on to a psycho-analysis.

Then I was glad that you brought up the subject of regression, which I was using rather loosely. I did just mention that the regression was not a simple return to infancy but contained the element of withdrawal and rather paranoid state needing a specialised protective environment. I do believe, however, that this can be said to be normal in a theoretical way if one refers to a very early stage of emotional development, something which is passed over and hardly noticed at the very beginning if all goes well. This is a matter for discussion, and it is exactly here that I am particularly interested in the subject.

In regard to the duration of the regression, I could not of course predict its length. I had indications, however, which perhaps are rather subtle, and I might have been absolutely wrong. I took as my main platform the relatively normal first two years, and following this the way in which the child dealt with the considerable environmental disturbances which started at the age of 2 by using the mother and by his technique of living in a slightly withdrawn state. In regard to this particular point I am now very much strengthened by my experience of having allowed a psycho-analytic patient to regress as far as was necessary. It did really happen that there was a bottom to the regression and no indication whatever of a need to return following the experience of having reached the bottom.

I would like to have had time to say these things but I think that the chairman was not at all helpful, otherwise he would have directed the discussion and you would have been called on at an earlier time. Next time I shall try to get you to someone to open the discussion so as to keep out the people who talk about watches and foetal hearts.

> Good wishes,
> Yours,
> D. W. Winnicott

P.S. I have just thought of the other point which was important. I agree with you that in ordinary analysis one tries to make it unnecessary for regression to have to take place, and one succeeds in the ordinary neurotic case. I do believe, however, that the experience of a few regressing cases enables one to see more clearly what to interpret. As an example I would say that since experiencing regressions I more often interpret to the patient in terms of need and less often in terms of wish. In many cases it seems to me sufficient that one says, for instance, "At this point you need me to see you this weekend," the implication being that from any point of view I can benefit from the weekend, which indirectly helps the patient, but from the patient's point of view at that particular moment there is nothing but harm from the existence of a gap in continuity of the treatment. If at such a moment one says "You would like me to give up my weekend" one is on the wrong track and one is in fact wrong. I expect you more or less agree with this too.

I would like to have had time to take up all these points.

1. Winnicott had read a paper entitled "The Management of a Case of Compulsive Thieving (Consideration of the Bearing of the Case, That Was Treated without Psycho-analysis, on a Psychoanalytic Theory)." Dr. Scott contributed to the discussion.

30 ᶒ To Esther Bick

11th June 1953.

Dear Mrs. Bick:

While I have your paper[1] in mind I would like to write you a word or two. I do hope that you will give a lot of thought to this idea of splitting and not take for granted that you are right. In your answer you talked about this woman's splitting mechanisms and used the word "she." She, by various means, cut and split objects. If the personality of this woman were split, you would not be able to use the word she in this simple way. It would almost seem as if you have not yet met someone fundamentally split. The gentleman who invented the word schizophrenia really did believe in the splitting of the personality, whereas it seems to me that you have got as far as seeing that a person who is whole can be concerned with dissociated elements in the inner and external world. I think this is rather an important point in view of the fact that in your use of the word splitting you are joining in with the current tendency . . . of the Klein grouping. In making this suggestion I was voicing the opinion usually unexpressed, of a large number in the Society.

You will understand that this is mostly a use of terms and there-fore is not very fundamental. Nevertheless it can be fundamental if those who use the word split in your way then proceed to feel that they have dealt with the true splitting of schizophrenics, which they have not done.

I am writing this to you because it arises out of your paper, which I found an interesting one, and you will understand that I would not criticise or appraise your paper on a detail like this.

In regard to further details, I really did mean that I think your term "regress to persecution" means nothing at all as it stands. I expect you will agree with me that this was some kind of short-hand that you have evolved and that you had not time to say what you were meaning. Actually I would be quite interested to know. I suppose you are referring to Melanie Klein's concept of a para-noid position in emotional development, which I consider to be one of her less well worked out theories, but in any case your term regression to persecution would not be able to convey any mean-ing to most of the people listening.

I think the chances are that the clue to your case is not yet in your hands. She has not yet lost the main symptom. I am sure that Melanie Klein is right that when you get through the quiet infancy period in the transference situation, biting will turn up instead of these magical cuttings by breath and flatus. I think that eventually you will be able to cover what is repressed by the word excite-ment, and then I think you will find that breathing excitement is the thing that the patient is trying to get to. This, as you know, is a very important part of sexual intercourse.

I am reminded of a case of compulsive over-breathing which came my way when I was a House Physician in 1922; this went on for many hours and was leading to serious physical effects, but it disappeared when in the history-taking I and the patient discov-ered that it started during intercourse and as part of a phobia of intercourse. I know that all this suffocation difficulty will be mixed up with body memories of the birth process but in my experience it is eventually the breathing at the climax of instinctual experience that is the thing that has to be found. I think that this mother, because she was depressed, took great care that her infant did not get excited, and of course in thinking this I am using the clinical notes that you gave.

There was a point which struck some of us, which was to do with a psychotic element in the patient's material. It had to do with her annihilation of you when she, according to your description, noticed everything in one corner of the room. I am thinking of what would happen if you were to give a long period without making interpretations, and perhaps you have done this; but it can easily be that by interpreting you reassure the patient against her anxiety of having annihilated you and that conversely, a period of leaving her alone would produce a severe anxiety attack which might have value in itself.

The paper certainly gives plenty of material for thought and discussion.

1. "Anxiety Underlying Phobia of Sexual Intercourse in a Woman."

31 ❧ *To Sylvia Payne*

7th October 1953.

Dear Dr. Payne:

I have taken rather longer than I meant to in answering your letter[1] . . .

I have found very great consternation in unexpected quarters when those who have taken part in the training scheme are dropped either partly or wholly. They do not like to ask why and they never actually find out, but they nearly always feel that they are no longer wanted for some reason or other. As you know from your intimate experience on all the Committees, the main difficulty is that the students are not able to give us sufficient time. We have tremendous teaching potential and we only use a little bit of it because the students are unable to be taught except in the evenings. This is a great loss to the teachers, teaching being something which develops unexpected qualities and which leads to very useful reorientations.

I personally am one of those who feel that I have been fairly seriously neglected as a teacher. The only teaching that I have ever done to students has been confined to the three lectures which I give to the third year students, and I certainly would not have been asked to give these. It was entirely my own suggestion. I used to give another small group of lectures but I saw that these had to be crowded out to make the training scheme less patchy and I gave them up voluntarily. The fact is that my own very considerable experience in the psycho-analysis of children has been absolutely wasted although as a matter of fact I have had more experience of long child analysis than almost anyone else. I realised a long time ago that I would not be asked to teach in the Society and therefore I concentrated on teaching teachers and I have had to develop my views through the 10 yearly lectures which I give at the Institute of Education as a result of Susan Isaac's original recommendation. I also give a large number of sporadic lectures all round the place which are based on personal reputation. In my own case I just simply understand that there is no time in the training scheme and my very big effort to work in something to do with child development this year is proving very difficult in practice.

. . . .

Yours sincerely,

D. W. Winnicott

1. Dr. Payne had written on behalf of a member of the Institute who was not asked to teach.

32 ⮡ *To David Rapaport*

9th October 1953

Dear Dr. Rapaport:

I am writing simply to let you know that I really did enjoy your talk on Wednesday and I felt that you really began to enable me to start giving my own ideas more in terms of psycho-analytic theory of an accepted kind. I am one of those people who feel compelled to work in my own way and to express myself in my own language first; by a struggle I sometimes come around to rewording what I am saying to bring it in line with other work, in which case I usually find that my own "original" ideas were not so original as I had to think they were when they were emerging. I suppose other people are like this too. I think I began to see where you and I would find a difference of opinion if we had time to talk.

I would like to feel that Masud Khan and yourself will give time for a discussion together. He is junior in the ordinary term as a psycho-analyst but I believe his knowledge of the literature and of the development of psycho-analytic thought is not equalled in our Society. If you and he are able to have a talk I shall personally benefit in an indirect way. It may be that there will be an opportunity for us to meet before you go back to U.S.A. but just in case the time passes and nothing has happened, I wish to let you know how very much I have enjoyed hearing you talk at the Wednesday meeting.

With good wishes,
Yours sincerely,
D. W. Winnicott

33 ❧ To Hannah Ries

27th November 1953.

Dear Mrs. Ries:

Your letter does not really need an answer but I felt like saying one thing, which is that I do not think it matters if Melanie Klein and particularly her followers have a phase in which they claim too much. I always remember the word "atom" which means that it cannot be split up. The physicists were great men and one cannot say that their work is no good because they thought the atom was the final dissection. In some places the followers of Mrs. Klein speak as if they knew everything, but in the course of time they will find that they do not.

I would like also to say that working with Mrs. Klein I have found that the work of Freud and the sort of work which you describe in your paper is not ignored, certainly by Mrs. Klein herself and people like Dr. Heimann. The trouble is that it is taken for granted in their writings and in their case descriptions, and people think that they are supplanting Freud's work by their own instead of enriching it. They are therefore to some extent responsible for the tremendous misunderstanding that exists at the present time in our Society. It is very easy to fall into this sort of error. I find myself that when I talk about regression and very early infantile problems people very easily think that I am unable to do an ordinary piece of analysis involving instincts and the ordinary work in the transference situation, which as a matter of fact I am all the time taking for granted, knowing that there is no point at all in going on to discover new things if one forgets the old things.

All this needs saying in our Society over and over again. I try very hard to put this point of view across in the three contacts that I have with the students each summer.

I think you will not mind my reminding you, because you know it already yourself, that the kind of analysis which you describe in your paper is applicable to the well-chosen neurotic case, the sort of case that Freud carefully chose to work on, although he sometimes got involved with psychotics almost against his will. This kind of analysis of interpersonal relationships does not cut any ice, as the saying is, in the analysis of psychotics or of the psychotic phases that can occur in normal people. You may disagree with this, and certainly there is plenty of room for argument, but the matter has great practical importance because there are fewer and fewer cases coming for analyses that are psychiatrically speaking neurotic cases. My own view is that it is the job of medically qualified analysts on the whole to tackle the analyses of psychotics, but of course non-medical analysts cannot avoid meeting from time to time psychotic phases in character analyses where there is no obvious psychotic label.

All this may not be entirely relevant to your letter or your paper but I feel like writing it to you. I shall be sorry if you retire to your consulting room and I do strongly suggest that you prepare yourself for the task of giving a new paper some time in the future.

> With very good wishes,
> Yours,
> D. W. Winnicott.

34 ⮞ *To W. Clifford M. Scott*

27th January 1954.

My dear Scott:

I want to let you know that I have enjoyed reading your paper. It seems to me that probably the groupings in the Society on the whole are grouped according to type of clinical case as well as according to viewpoint. I myself find several direct connections between your paper and my work. Probably I shall think of some more constructive things to say about your paper in the course of time but the bit that I cannot agree with is your assumption about sleep. I feel that there is so very much more to be said about sleep that the little bit of truth in your "regression to sleep" reference gets lost. I doubt whether sleep is even the right word; at any rate I think that the sleep you are talking about is extremely unlike the sort of sleep that most of us have at night in which any dissociation between sleeping and waking is very markedly lessened by the dream that we more or less remember on waking, even if only for a second. The sort of sleep that you are referring to seems to me to be more of the nature of a depersonalisation or an extreme dissociation or something awfully near to the unconsciousness belonging to a fit.

I know that you have good clinical evidence for everything you say. Nevertheless I want to let you know that it is just at the point of your mentioning the word sleep that I get a jolt. At the same time I do not think that your idea is entirely wrong. As an example, I believe, of the sort of way in which these things can appear clinically, I would give that of a patient of mine who is dangerous just after expressing genuine love. In fact it was necessary for me over a long period of time to hold this patient's hands throughout the analysis, this being the equivalent of certifying her and putting her in a padded cell for the analytic hour. In this way she was able to proceed and to express love and hate. If I failed in this physical way then in actual practice I got hit and hurt and this did no good either to me or to the patient. In this case the oscillation between love and hate seemed to me to have been almost measurable but what is more important they were painful to the patient.

I could give other examples, and the one I think of immediately is that of children who are helped rather than hindered by being told that they fear madness, the madness they fear being this oscillation between love and hate.

I would very much like to have been at the discussion and certainly I would have welcomed your putting forward these ideas which are fresh and which even if wrong are stimulating and remind us of the relationship between psycho-analysis and psychiatry and biology.

It was very good indeed of you to come and see me the other day. I am now, I suppose, well, but I am staying in bed a few days longer than necessary.

> Every good wish,
> Yours,
> D. W. Winnicott.

35 ❧ To W. Clifford M. Scott

26th February 1954.

My dear Scott:

I think I am rather bad at making use of questions at the end of a paper and I have had explained to me what you said which I could not understand at the time. In fact I believe I did you an injustice implying that you were considering the hurrying up of analyses which you were not intending to imply. What you said simply made me think of the sort of answer I gave about getting into touch with processes.

I think that you were referring to the fact that I had not made clear where I would come to differ from Melanie Klein and it was a terrible lapse that I miscalculated the time and chose to cut out the more definite statement of difference of opinion. I think you were probably giving me the chance if I could take it to state that there is a gradual process in the infant whereby the various capacities come together and make possible the depressive position achievement. By contrast some of the Klein writings seem to give highly organised processes a place in very early infancy where they can be only present at moments or sporadically without a relationship to the total individual.

I am sure I have not got it right but what I am trying to say is that I do realise that I was rather stupid about what you said. I am told by some that they felt that what you said was very clear. It may be that you will have time to do as you sometimes do and dictate a version of it to your secretary for my benefit.

Good wishes,
Yours,
D. W. Winnicott.

36 ᷞ *To Anna Freud*

18th March 1954.

Dear Miss Freud,

It was good of you to write and I am sure we all missed you at the meeting. My paper produced a really interesting discussion I believe. My aim will be now to try to correlate my ideas with those of Kris and Hartmann[1] as I feel what they have recently written that we are all trying to express the same things, only I have an irritating way of saying things in my own language instead of learning how to use the terms of psycho-analytic metapsychology.

I am trying to find out why it is that I am so deeply suspicious of these terms. Is it because they can give the appearance of a common understanding when such understanding does not exist? Or is it because of something in myself? It can, of course, be both.

Good wishes,
Yours sincerely,
D. W. Winnicott.

1. Ernst Kris and Heinz Hartmann were at the forefront of the field of ego psychology.

37 ⮤ *To Betty Joseph*

Dear Betty Joseph:

You will probably be surprised to find a third letter from me on the subject of your taking the trouble to speak after my Regression paper. This letter is stimulated by a note from Dr. Scott in which he goes over the whole discussion.

It seems to me that there are two points worth going further into. One of these has to do with the idea of a bad environment, or in your sort of language, a bad breast. I will talk about Scott's question which he says results from your remarks: "Cannot any bad experience be made worse by the patient's fantasy?" I think that there is a confusion here which is my fault. The thing is that you and I would not disagree if we are talking about fantasy of a bad (or a good) breast. What I am trying to point out is not the fantasy of a good or bad breast. I am trying to draw attention to the very early stages, quite apart from the fantasy. I think that these two things are as different from each other as two things can be. If we mix them up we shall certainly get into a muddle. I find it very difficult to get people to leave for a moment the infant's fantasy of a bad breast and to go a stage further back to the effect of a bad mothering technique, such as for instance rigidity (mother's defence against hate) or muddle (expression of mother's chaotic state). If you feel that it is not possible for a mothering technique to affect an infant except in so far as an infant has a fantasy of the mother or of the part object, then I think you must say so, and it is an interesting point of view of an extreme kind. I am certainly claiming that the two subjects are separated and must be considered in different ways.

The second point is expressed by Scott: "What happens to the bad breast in the good state of regression?" I think I dealt with this in my first letter when I was saying that I was trying to get to something earlier than the presentation of what can be felt by the infant as a bad or a good breast. Nevertheless I did deal with the fact that the bad mothering technique comes out with extreme clearness in the sort of treatment that I was describing in my paper. I want to emphasize what I wrote before which is that the bad mothering is an essential thing in the sequence in the technique that I described and I tried to point out that the way in which after a good experience which corrects the original bad one the next thing is that the patient uses one's failures and in this way brings into the present each original mothering technique inadequacy.

Do not be perturbed by this sequence of letters from me; you will understand that I am simply talking to myself in terms of writing round to those who did my paper the honour of discussing it.

Yours very sincerely,
D. W. Winnicott.

38 ஃ *To W. Clifford M. Scott*

13th April 1954.

My dear Scott:

I am very happy to have your comments on my Regression paper[1] and the discussion so that I can study them. So far I have only read them through once or twice and I find a great deal to think about. At the present minute I would like to make one or two comments.

In regard to the point that you make about regression as the reverse of a process you will have noticed that before I read the paper I altered the word "process" to "progress." This alters your criticism, I think. There is progress and regression and as I tried to point out in my paper, for regression there has to be a rather complicated ego organisation. I suggest that the word reversal is not so bad when applied to the word progress, whereas I agree that it is not sensible when applied to the word process.

I would agree to use your words "Regression is an attempt to use previous types of behaviour normal or abnormal as a defence against present conflict" only there is so much more to be said that needs saying. It seems to me that we really agree on this point since my alteration meets your statement that reversal should be kept for attempts on the part of the patient to reverse something, for instance, growth. This is exactly what I mean.

When you compare impulses and wishes with needs I think you are exactly stating the change of outlook that I am asking for. It seems to be very difficult for me to get analysts to look at early infancy except in terms of impulses and wishes. I think that Betty Joseph in particular represents the point of view which takes wishes as the beginning of everything. I can agree with all she says about good and bad breasts and the fact that a bad breast is a fantasy of the infant; even when using judgment we can say a mother is failing. What I am referring to, however, has nothing to do with this at all; it has to do with the earlier or more primary mothering techniques which if inadequate fail to meet needs and therefore disturb the continuity of development of the individual.

In regard to the failure situation there is a great deal that I do not understand and I am sure it is not covered by the word inhibition and that rage and depression refer to defensive techniques which also belong to a later stage of development. There is no state of frustration because the individual has not yet become able to stay frustrated. The failure situation as I am referring to it results in a massive reaction to impingement; at the same time something that could have become the individual becomes hidden away; hidden where I cannot say but separated off and protected from further impingement by the developing false self which is reactive as a main feature.

I expect all this has been said before but I cannot find where it has been said in reference to the very beginning where I think it belongs and I believe that our difficulties in the classification of psychological disorders in young children and indeed in infants is due to the fact that we have not yet made full use of this concept of the false self developing reactively and more and more hiding the true impulsive self which might under more favourable circumstances have been gathering strength through experience on a non-reactive basis.

In the recovery of the original failure situation when the frozen failure situation becomes unfrozen then the individual for the first time can feel frustrated and can develop more complex defences as well as experiencing rage or even anger directed towards the exact failure.

By surrender I am not meaning identification. There is something that I have found in my work towards the recovery of these patients when after tremendously careful testing the mothering technique is handed over to the analyst and what I have called the true self comes out of safe hiding, to use my grownup fantasy, and risks living in the new environment which I am able to provide, at any rate in token form in the analytic setting.

There is one point that I would like to make particularly clear. In my paper I certainly failed to give the right impression about interpretation. I wrongly assumed that it would be understood that the whole analysis has been carried along by correct interpretations each one of which is absolutely vital. I suppose there has been one of those vital interpretations either every day, or every few days as when there has been a phase that had to be first acted out without interpretation, neither the patient nor myself knowing what was going to turn up. When I said that I only made one interpretation I meant of instinct in the transference as when early on in the analysis I interpreted ordinary oral interest. The point was that this would have been a correct interpretation in an ordinary analytic case but here it meant that I had been seduced by the false self. There had of course been no instinct related to the true self and it must have been a matter of some years before the patient had surrendered or started to live her own life taking the risk as to whether I could manage or could not manage the mothering technique which had failed in the first instance. I am hoping in the printed version of the paper to make it quite clear that my interpretations all along were of vital importance, each time relieving what appeared to be a block in progress.

There is a great deal more in your comments that I will try and study and possibly I will be writing you again. In any case it was very kind of you to take all the trouble and also to be supportive on the actual night on which I was reading the paper.

Incidentally, I have only just found the letter in your envelope which referred to the Publication Committee's decision. I am very glad that my papers are to be published and I will prepare them as soon as I possibly can. In regard to the book that I have nearly written, I think I have decided to ask the Tavistock Publications to deal with this. It certainly is for the professional public, as Dr. Jones hoped. In regard to the more popular papers I am trying to bring out immediately another book which collects together the two pamphlets and other papers written for mothers and teachers and the like.

I hope your family will all have a happy Easter holiday.

Yours,

D. W. Winnicott.

1. "Metapsychological and Clinical Aspects of Regression within the Psycho-Analytical Setup."

39 ⮬ *To Sir David K. Henderson*

10th May 1954.

Dear Sir David:

I enjoyed reading your lecture as reported in the B.M.J. in one of the recent numbers. There are two points which I would like to take up for comment, and if you agree to read what I write I hope you will understand that the main thing I have in mind is that your lecture was up to the usual high standard of what comes from you yourself and that it has value because of your wide experience and important position.

One point that I felt like writing to you about was the matter of the lay psycho-therapist. I do see the point that the fact that there is a big demand for psycho-therapy should not lead to any panic provision of half-trained psycho-therapists. We are always up against the same problem at the Institute of Psycho-Analysis where we are asked to give a shorter course in our training or to give lectures on psycho-therapy without insisting on a personal analysis. As you probably know, the policy of the Institute is to resist this sort of argument. Nevertheless I do want to suggest that the medical profession has already missed the boat in regard to the matter of psycho-therapy. It is now too late to adopt a policy that only medical men and women should be trained. I believe you may be able to agree with me that psychiatrists have been, if anything, slightly more resistant to the idea of psycho-therapy than other doctors have, and in some form or other all of us are to blame for the present position.

I would very much like you to consider whether you are not able, should an occasion arise, to support the idea of a properly trained lay psycho-analyst who gives an absolute undertaking not to take medical responsibility and to treat only patients who are sponsored by a physician, if possible by a psychiatrist.

It is not only in the matter of child psycho-therapy where some development of this kind is inevitable, because there are very few medical men and women who will take the trouble to undergo the training which has to follow the long training in medicine, but it also applies to the psycho-therapy of adults, and many adults coming to analysis can be sent to a lay analyst on the grounds that they are not grossly disturbed in a psychiatric sense and that they are not seriously ill physically. As a matter of fact a medically qualified psycho-analyst does not usually find it a good idea to manage the mental hospital and the specialist medical aspects of the awkward phases in an analysis, and during such phases seeks the co-operation of a colleague just as the lay analyst needs to do.

I know that the discussion of this matter has many sides to it but I would very much like to feel that you in your important position have considered the problem in this sort of way. You will understand that I am writing quite personally and not as an official at the Institute of Psycho-Analysis.

The other point is similar. It concerns your reference to child psychiatry and paediatrics. Here I feel that you might have mentioned my name when you mentioned [Leo] Kanner. It is not, I can assure you, that I am interested in having my own name put forward (and I think you will really believe this, otherwise I would not mention this point) but I cannot see why it is we must go to America for something that exists in our own country. I believe you know that I am a paediatrician and represent a link in this country between paediatrics and child psychiatry. There are others, such as Mildred Creak and [Kenneth] Cameron at the Maudsley who contribute as much as Kanner has done, although in a less spectacular manner, but they are not really deeply rooted in paediatrics as I myself have been. I feel this matter very strongly and agree fully with you when you deplore the extreme reluctance of paediatrics to give to child psychiatry its due and to see that half of paediatrics is child psychiatry. The Professors of Paediatrics are called Professors of Child Health and this causes the utmost confusion since not one of them, not even my friend R. W. B. Ellis of your own city, really knows what psycho-analysis is. Moreover what you say about paediatrics and child psychiatry could also be said about gynaecology in so far as the gynaecologist with the maternity nurse is responsible for the initiation of infant feeding.

There is a new friendliness in paediatrics toward child psychiatry but this does not go very deep in regard to understanding. The whole time we are up against the reluctance to give psycho-analysis its place as something corresponding to physiology and anatomy in relation to physical medicine.

In this second group of remarks that I am making you will see that I am welcoming what you have said and trying to inform you that a big effort is being made at the present time to bring about a better relationship.

There is an interesting Congress due in Stockholm in September on this very subject, called together by W.H.O., and a preliminary Conference was held in Geneva a year ago.

In the end as I am writing this letter I am not exactly sure of my purpose, but I do know that I feel that I want to associate myself with the general tendency of your remarks in your interesting lecture.

Yours sincerely,
D. W. Winnicott.

40 ཞ་ To John Bowlby

11th May 1954.

Dear Bowlby:

In my contacts I come up against quite a lot of people who are worried about the way your work has been used by those who want to close down Day Nurseries.[1] As you know, there is a good deal of emotion engendered in all these matters, and one has to allow for all this. On the other hand, I feel that you would like to know what is going on and I am sure you have been given this information by other people.

You will probably agree with me, and I would very much like to be able to say in a public discussion that you agree, that there is a deplorable shortage of Day Nurseries accommodation. Nursery School accommodation is of course short at the moment because of the bulge in the number of children at the older age group. There ought also to be a building programme of Nursery Schools, but these are other matters and concern the Ministry of Education. In regard to Day Nurseries, however, which are part of the Ministry of Health obligations, there is only accommodation for certain priorities, and not nearly enough. Moreover, the relief which ordinary normal mothers can get from making use of a Day Nursery when they go for part-time work is non-existent because of the priorities and the insistence of full-time work when there happens to be a Day Nursery available. What in fact happens is that mothers needing help put their children out with unqualified and unregistered foster parents, and the closing of Day Nurseries certainly would not increase the amount that mothers are able to have children at home.

I saw a mother this week who is not very good with her own child but who has had 52 foster-children. She may have done a good job but all these children would have been better off in a good Day Nursery.

This is a vital problem and I am afraid that at the moment your having been quoted in connection with the closing down of Day Nurseries is doing harm to the very valuable tendency of your argument. I wonder if there is anything you can do about this. A letter to the press disclaiming your interest in the closing down of Day Nurseries would make a lot of difference.

You will understand that if we accept the fact of Day Nurseries, I would agree if you were to say that in many of them there is a very great deal to be learned in regard to the care of small children. I would add that in the Day Nursery world psychology has turned up in recent years although not in any way comparable to the very interesting work which forms the basis of the Nursery School.

Perhaps when we meet you could let me know in a few words your feelings about these matters.

Yours,
D. W. Winnicott.

1. Dr. Bowlby's pioneering work on the ill effects of separation from their mothers on young children was being used to argue for the closing down of day nurseries.

41 ಇ *To Klara Frank*

20th May 1954.

Dear Dr. Frank:

The meeting was so late last night that I was not able to go to Dr. Lantos' afterwards; I find that very late nights make the next day's work impossible. I am therefore writing to say that I enjoyed your paper and I thought that it was a very useful and honest case description.

You added a very great deal to your case by letting us know that the patient does not acknowledge feeling happy. In my opinion this made sense of the case and certainly it in no way spoiled the feeling that we got about the work done in the three years of the treatment.

I think you will understand that your title "A Case of Over Indulgence" was responsible for drawing us towards the interplay of the mother and child factors in the early stages of this patient's development. I feel that there is a great deal here that you could tell us if we could have drawn you out. By a certain date I suppose in the childhood of this patient it could be said that the mother was over indulging because of the special needs of her child.

Before that date one would have to say that the mother was in some way prevented from enjoying a simple straightforward love-hate relationship with her child, and through the difficult times that she was in and through the fact of its being her last child she was compelled to exaggerate the giving aspect of the relationship, and leaving out some of the other tremendously important things about mothering. For instance, the patient's symptom of not knowing what to do with her hands seems to me to be likely to be associated with the mother's inability to wait for the infant to create out of need by hand exploration. Satisfaction came too early, too quickly, and too well, and in this respect one can say that the infant's hands were cut off in respect of their creativity.

I was longing for you to tell us more about this child's use of dolls and teddies and objects and the whole matter of what (as you know) I have termed the transitional phenomena of her early infancy. The impression given is that the mother placed herself in the position of a transitional object and deprived the child of the very great value to be got from the use of substitute objects, this being to some extent dependent upon frustration, well-timed, and following on a good enough adaptation in the very early phases.

I hope you will not mind my writing like this but I am trying to show you that the case interested me more than I was able to express. I would say that you were not able to give a very clear picture of the analysis and the specific points of management in the daily sessions. I think if you had been able to do so we should have been shown that you were having to adopt a technique which belongs to the management of an antisocial case although here the antisocial illness was manageable and certainly, as speakers pointed out, not different from what might be found in a very large number of people who go for normal. I think that you will probably agree that in the three years available for treatment the patient was not able to reach in the transference the primitive ruth-less oral love relationship which would provide the only sensible basis for guilt and for the reparation, which she finds herself caught up in without being able to link them consciously with the original ruthless attack on the mother.

Yours very sincerely,
D. W. Winnicott.

42 &ved; *To Sir David K. Henderson*

20th May 1954.

Dear Professor Henderson,

I am grateful to you for the fact that you took the trouble to answer my letter in such detail. The nature of your reply seems to allow me to write to you again.[1]

We are corresponding on two topics and first I would like to say some more about lay psycho-therapy. I cannot help agreeing with a great deal that you have written but I think that although it is not possible to control the analyses done by lay analysts, or by any other analyst, it is possible and it should be increasingly possible, to control the type of case that is sent to the lay analyst. Diagnosis is a matter of extreme difficulty in these matters, as I need hardly point out to yourself, and many acutely ill patients are not so fundamentally in danger, whereas seemingly less ill patients may have very powerful defence organisations and may turn out in analysis eventually to be extremely ill at core. There will always be mistakes and it will be necessary to tolerate the fact that the lay analysts will acutely need the psychiatrists' help at certain moments, and sometimes will have to hand over a case to the psychiatrist because of failure. Failures are so common, however, in any attempt to treat a mental patient that it should be easily possible to weigh up the failures against the successes. It may be that lay analysts have not yet any successes to claim; I would nevertheless support their training and their being used in carefully selected cases or else in work in institutions where the total responsibility is shared in any case. I think it will be wasteful if we look at the matter in twenty years' time to have all the psycho-therapy done by fully trained psychiatrists, and certainly there will never be enough psychiatrists available to meet one-tenth of the acute need or a thousandth part of the sub-acute need.

Incidentally, I find that some of the failures that people note and put down to psycho-analysis turn out to be failures of those who have not been trained in psycho-analysis, and from my point of view this makes a tremendous difference. It does not alter the fact, however, that the failures in psycho-therapy fall to the lot of analysts, however well trained.

Where I am in very full agreement with you is in the paragraph in which you describe your dislike of the analyst who will not concern himself with environmental features. I personally have never been one of this kind and I cannot understand this attitude except that while psycho-analysis is learning its job there must be a concentration on one aspect. No doubt analysts have felt that they had enough on hand to deal with the patient and this is often sufficient when the patient is not of a mental hospital type. In the last decade a great deal of work has been done amongst analysts on the way in which the environment is increasingly important in the actual analysis of borderline cases and it is merely a matter of time before psycho-analysis as a whole concerns itself with the whole aspect of the management problem, and this without abandoning the main principles of the psycho-analytic technique.

In regard to my own work, I really have always done a great deal along management lines, and this of course could not be avoided in child psychiatry since in child work one is dealing with the whole population and therefore with the potential mental hospital case along with the neurotics and the potential psychosomatics. I am just like other doctors in being able to say that I have had about twenty thousand personal cases and I mention this to show that obviously a great deal has come my way which has nothing to do with being an analyst. What is more important, however, is that in the analysis of borderline cases I have been able to make my little contribution towards the new developments whereby the whole environmental care becomes interwoven in with the analytic work.

I would like to refer a little also to the second part, and I feel a little bit ashamed about having put my criticism that way, in the form of a question as to why my name should not be mentioned. Nevertheless I think that a great deal of the work of [Leo] Kanner has become important because of the organisation which has been possible there. I would find it very difficult myself to mention one single point in which Kanner has contributed to our knowledge of the emotional development of the child, and therefore of the adult. The most important work in regard to the emotional development of the child has been done in this country and is being done here. That which is being done in America is largely an offshoot of the work that clusters around the name of Anna Freud and from my point of view the major developments are in psycho-analysis which is the physiology and anatomy of psychiatry, or shall I say of psycho-therapy. Very considerable advances in both theory and practice have been made in London. Mildred Creak and [Kenneth] Cameron are not analysts but they are contributing in their own way. Naturally from your association with Kanner you would wish to mention his name and I would be sorry if you left it out, but it seems to me strange that with your very wide knowledge of psychiatry in this country you seem to be out of touch with the good work which I really do claim has come from this country and from no other.

There is one point also which I would like to add. In regard to beds for child psychiatry, I have never believed that these should be in any kind of a hospital. Even Cameron at the Maudsley modifies the hospital routine toward that of the small hostel group. It is most unsatisfactory having child psychiatric cases in any institution. On the other hand all of us make very great use of small groupings, (usually not small enough unfortunately) whereby antisocial and psychotic children can be cared for in small family units. We learned a great deal about this in the war and I wrote a paper[2] at the end of the war pointing out the way in which the hostels for evacuated children had been extremely important for the child psychiatrists who were able to use them for the management and often the successful treatment of various types of psychotic child case. Moreover the vast majority of childhood psychotic phases are seen through in the child's own family and ought not to be seen through in any other way.[3]

1. In Professor Henderson's reply to Winnicott's letter of May 10, he had emphasized the problems inherent in lay analysis, including what he believed to be the impossibility of providing adequate supervision.
2. "Children's Hostels in War and Peace."
3. The rest of this letter is missing.

43 ❧ To Anna Freud and Melanie Klein

3rd June 1954.

Dear Miss Freud, Mrs. Klein:

This letter follows on the remark that I made somewhat clumsily at the meeting on Monday when yourself, Mrs. Klein and Dr. Payne attended a Council meeting by invitation. I am writing because I feel rather strongly on the matter that I raised. I want to draw attention to the effect of the official grouping. I am thinking of the health of the British Psycho-Analytical Society and trying to look into the future.

My suggestion is that it is not only true to say that the A and B groupings were essential 10 years ago and that the adoption of these groupings saved the Society from splitting, but that it is also true that at the present time the reason for this arrangement has ceased, that is to say, there is no danger whatever of the expulsion of those who follow Miss Freud. Neither is it true that either group is likely to walk out; the Society has now settled down like any other society to the fact that there are scientific differences which automatically clear up in the course of time just as other and new differences appear.

There is a comment that I would like to make at this point which is that there is a slight but interesting difference between the formation of the two groupings. In the case of Mrs. Klein's colleagues and friends it is true, whether by chance or otherwise, that inclusion in the group depends on the fact of having analysis from Mrs. Klein or an analysand of Mrs. Klein or an analysand of such an analysand. The only exception that I know of is Mrs. Riviere and I know of no analyst who has completed an analysis in the Klein group who is not included by Mrs. Klein as a Klein follower. In the case of Miss Freud's followers, the matter is more one of a type of education and it happens that this gives a less rigid boundary. One could say that whereas the followers of Mrs. Klein are all children and grandchildren, the followers of Miss Freud all went to the same school. I mention this difference in the formation of the two groups as I think it produces its own complications and contributes to the false view which the newcomer to psychoanalysis gets through being told of the two groups.

The idea that certain analysts are more likely than others to express Mrs. Klein's views accurately and that certain other analysts are more likely to express Miss Freud's views accurately can be accepted easily and it is to be hoped that this state of affairs will continue and that other members of the Society will also have those who are closely in touch with their individual point of view. Also that there will be overlap and no rigid line between those who accurately interpret and those who are not qualified to represent the analyst in question. There is no doubt that for some time to come there will be no-one of comparable importance in this respect to your two selves and I can see no reason why the abolition of the idea of named groupings that are officially recognised would alter procedure. The teaching programme would remain, balanced as at present, for some years, and we have no right to legislate for the future. Incidentally, if we in the present try to set up rigid patterns we thereby create iconoclasts or claustrophobics (perhaps I am one of them) who can no more stand the falsity of a rigid system in psychology than they can tolerate it in religion.

In writing this letter I am concerned with the future and with the fact that any one of us may die. I consider it to be of absolutely vital importance to the future of the Society that both of yourselves shall break up the groupings in so far as they are official. No one can break them up except yourselves and you can only do this while you are alive. If it should happen that you should die, then the grouping which is officially recognised in the nomenclature will become absolutely rigid and it will be a generation or more before the Society can recover from this disaster which will be a clumping based not on science but on personalities or even I might say on politics since the original groupings were justifiable but defensive constructs.

I have no reason to think that I shall live longer than either of yourselves but I find the prospect of having to deal with the rigid groupings that would become automatically established at the death of either of yourselves one which appalls me.

This matter is so important that if there is something about my manner which is irritating I hope you will not let it stand in the way of an objective review of the whole situation. I am trying very hard not to let my own peculiarities confuse the issue but if I have not succeeded may I remind you that there is still the issue itself and that the Society as it is at present only makes sense if it is the basis for a developing scientific Society which will go on serving the cause of science and the study of human nature. I know that in saying this I am uttering a platitude; we all agree about it. Nevertheless it occurs to me that the point that I have raised may not have been sufficiently understood.

Speaking as Training Secretary over the past three years I can say that my task would have been easier had there been no official recognition of groupings and as far as I can see there would have been no difference at all in regard to the placing of candidates who usually express their preference for a close association with one or another of yourselves (i.e. if they know anything about it) and who are not helped but are confused by the fact that it is necessary to give official recognition to what amounts to differences in the scientific field and not to political organisations which 10 years ago, but not now, were defensible.

I am addressing this letter to yourselves and sending a copy to Dr. Sylvia Payne. Apart from this there is no-one who knows of this letter and I think this is of extreme importance because, should you decide to abolish the ideal of official recognition of the two groups, this idea should come from yourselves.[1]

Yours sincerely,
D. W. Winnicott.

1. Both Mrs. Klein and Miss Freud rejected Winnicott's plea. They regarded the division in the British Institute as still necessary for proper training conditions.

44 ?~ *To Michael Fordham*

11th June 1954.
Dear Fordham:

It was extremely kind of you to write me at length.[1] I always admire people like yourself who really seem to read other people's papers; so very often I postpone reading something which is at all near my own subject because of the slight warp that it gives to the development of original ideas. When I have got something published, however, I then like to read around it. This is a rather weak policy but I must admit to it.

There is only one comment, which is about your feeling that I have said something to upset religious people in the paper in the B.J.M.P.[2] If you look at this again I do not believe that you will be able to substantiate your suggestion. One must be able to look at religious beliefs and their place in psychology without being considered to be antagonistic to anyone's personal religion. I have found others who thought that I was anti-religious in some of my writings but it has always turned out that what they were annoyed about was that I was not myself religious in their own particular way.

Let me know if you really fundamentally think that I am wrong.

Yours,
D. W. Winnicott.

1. Fordham, a leading Jungian, had written about Winnicott's paper on the depressive position. He found numerous parallels between Winnicott's thought and Jung's,

although he criticized what he took to be the suggestion that art and religion were merely "spare time amusements."

2. *British Journal of Medical Psychology.*

45 ᴥ *To Harry Guntrip*

20th July 1954.

Dear Mr. Guntrip,

You will hardly believe it, but it is only now that I have been able to get down to reading your letter which you kindly wrote after reading my paper on Regression.[1] I find the points that you made extremely interesting and also I am trying to profit by your interest in relating new ideas to the work of Fairbairn.

There seems to be just one thing that you have taken from Fairbairn which I think is unnecessary, and that is the tendency to think of his work as opposed to that of Freud. You remember that in his book he makes a very definite point of supplanting Freud's theories and in my opinion he spoils a very good book by this, which is quite unnecessary. From my point of view any theories that I may have which are original are only valuable as a growth of ordinary Freudian psycho-analytic theory. My paper on Regression would make no sense at all if planted on a world that had not been prepared for it by Freud. In any paper I have written I simply take for granted that people know their Freud and are familiar with the developing theory which had to be started off somewhere. Freud could easily have gone straight through intuitively to fundamental truths but that was not what he wanted to do. He wanted to set aside all sorts of tempting intuitions (which however turned up in the footnotes and odd remarks here and there) and he wanted to begin a new science, although this meant concentrating on the bit of work that was just under his nose at the time.

I would very much like to know that you feel in this way about Freud's work to which we all owe everything if we are doing psycho-therapy. I also feel that Fairbairn must really agree with all this, only he happens to take the line that he is knocking Freud over and putting up something in his place.

Apart from this detail I am most gratified from your letter to find that you are really understanding the sort of things I am trying to say. I should be very glad to have the chance of reading the account that you have written of a case. I am hoping that my regression article will be published shortly in the International Journal of Psycho-Analysis.

Yours sincerely,
D. W. Winnicott, F.R.C.P.

1. Winnicott had sent this paper to Guntrip at the request of W. R. D. Fairbairn, a Scottish analyst with whom Guntrip had been in treatment. Fairbairn was a member of the Middle Group and contributed a powerfully original theory of emotional development.

46 ⮞ To *The Editor, the* Times

21st July 1954.

Sir,

Sponsored Television,

As sponsored television gradually comes nearer I find an acute need in myself to see a statement of my own point of view written out in a public place. It is the point of view of an ordinary thinking and feeling Englishman, living in his own country, and blessed or cursed with a sense of values.

We need not go to U.S.A. We only need to tune in to Radio Luxembourg to hear what sponsoring means. Those who like being urged to wash their whites whiter or to rinse their kidneys cleaner (by using this and that) are welcome to this vehicle for culture. For myself, being allergic to propaganda of all kinds, I know I shall hate politicians with increasing hatred as I gradually see a new generation growing up taking for granted the advertisers' right to intrude.

A Public Relations Officer of the T.V. Advertisers' Guild will surely answer this letter and will very politely show me to be wrong, if possible by statistical method. I am inviolate, however, since I am a mature person giving an opinion, and I and my opinion are not for seduction. Along with thousands of others I absolutely loathe what is coming and shall never forgive the politicians who are responsible.

Of course it will be done very nicely. Gems of music, plays and art will be given us, but the matrix will be toothpaste; not the best toothpaste, but the one which is most persistently to be pushed.

> Yours etc.
> D. W. Winnicott.

47 ᘛ *To Harry Guntrip*

13th August 1954.

Dear Dr. Guntrip,

I am grateful to you for letting me see your paper: "Analysis Blocked. . . .etc." There is much in this paper that I like. I am sure that something had to be done in the analysis of this patient of yours in addition to the giving of correct interpretations at the right moments. There are probably borderline cases, perhaps commonly so, in which it is possible to avoid action by appropriate interpretation, but even so there are, I am sure, many cases in which some action such as you describe is necessary. In the more severe cases this probably becomes the main thing over a phase. Some people think that analysis has been abandoned when the analyst acts so, but I am sure that these people fail with analyses that could have succeeded. I would very much like to have a talk with you some time or other about this business of the introjection of the bad object. I find that your outlook is very much influenced by Fairbairn, and understandably so, but I do invite you to have a look into this matter of your relation to psychoanalysis in general, so that you can have your own relationship and not Fairbairn's. Just as Fairbairn presents his work, as I said in my last letter, in a way which makes it look as if he is all the time supplanting Freud, so he also I suggest talks as if he were supplanting Melanie Klein. For instance, this matter of the introjection of the bad object is quite clear in Melanie Klein's work. The bad situation or object or relationship is taken in for purposes of being controlled. This is an example of a magical introjection and sometimes introjected bad situations take over control for a short time or else become reprojected with the result that the patient has delusions of a certain type, but in the same way there is also the healthy capacity for the introjection of good objects and relationships and situations.

It seems to me that it is impossible to jump from the recognition of the introjection of bad objects to the idea that the original introjection is of the bad rather than the good object. In any case this tenet of theory bypasses the more important matter of the origin of internal objects by less magical methods; I mean the ordinary incorporation associated with oral experience where the incorporating is merely the imaginative elaboration of a bodily function. According to Melanie Klein the basic build-up of the inner world is through oral experience, although of course in this case the resulting internal objects are not recognisable because they really have been eaten up. The inner world grows on these experiences as the body grows on the food ingested.

Perhaps you can see from this why it is I feel that Fairbairn again spoils his own good work by making a point of disagreeing with Melanie Klein over an unimportant matter. It is indeed remarkable that Fairbairn has managed to make his positive contribution when out of touch with the main body of analysts through his living in Edinburgh. For my own part I feel that the disadvantage of his being out of touch is that he has not been able to see how far he is playing a part in the development of theory, a process which is going on all the time in the Society but which gets into the literature ten years late.

I am enclosing, in case you would like to read it, an article of mine that seems to have a bearing on your patient's separation of the head from the body. I have come across this a good deal, especially in one patient, and I have found that the fundamental thing is not the separation of head and body but the separation of mind from psyche-soma. You may be able to gather this from the paper I am lending you, but it is a matter that wants writing up more clearly.

In regard to the future of your woman patient, I certainly think that you are on the right road but that there are difficulties ahead. For instance, you have been able to follow the patient's regression to dependence and to be in the place of an early mother figure, that is to say one that is prior to the patient's objectively perceived mother. I would think that there may be very great hate of you because of this position that you have taken as the patient emerges from the regression and therefore becomes aware of the dependence. If one is not expecting this one may be puzzled at the tremendous hate which turns up within the love relationship in these regressed states.

There is certainly a great deal that could be discussed that has a relation to both our papers. I think you will not mind my saying what I said again about Fairbairn's attitude, as you have obviously got a very great deal that is valuable from Fairbairn and there is no reason for you to take over his rather special attitude about the relationship of his work to that of Freud and Klein.

Good wishes and many thanks,

Yours sincerely,
D. W. Winnicott.

48 ⮞ *To Roger Money-Kyrle*

23rd September 1954.

My dear Money-Kyrle:

I found myself getting annoyed talking to you last night and I do not want to leave it like that as I have a great respect for you and not a little affection.

I think what irritated me was that I faintly detected in your attitude this matter of the party line, a matter to which I am allergic. Your own opinion is what I asked for. The father of the child being in analysis with you, it seemed good to ask whether you want to be involved or not in the choice of analyst. If you do not want to be involved, then I will do as I have been used to doing over a period of more than twenty years, which is to use my own judgment. My own judgment is based not on what people write in papers but on the experience of a lot of cases referred and treated. When people like Marion Milner, or myself for that matter, write papers, we do not write them in order to show each time that we have grasped Mrs. Klein's contributions to theory, but we write them because of an original idea which needs ventilating.

I think one day soon we ought to meet and talk about these matters, because if you think that someone like Dr. Segal, who is just starting analysis of children, is in the same street as Marion Milner who has a vast experience, there is something fundamentally different in our attitudes and it would be interesting to talk about those differences.

At the moment there is something much more simple in hand. I want to get this child to an analyst that I know can do the work, and who also is acceptable to yourself. I have asked you about Marion Milner and I am waiting for your reply. I shall not mind at all if you say that you do not want her as this child's analyst. There is no need for you to give any reason. Incidentally, I asked Dr. Munro first, but she has no room in which to do analysis of a child, unfortunately.

> Good wishes,
> Yours,
> D. W. Winnicott.

49 ও To D. Chaplin

18th October 1954.

Dear Miss Chaplin,

The problem you raise[1] is a very interesting one and I know that it has been in the back of our minds often when we have been talking generally or specifically about cases. I think there is an answer to the question you raise which does not in fact alter either your view or mine, but this is a matter for discussion and it is always possible that I use the word psychotic in a way that is not justifiable. I have this constantly under review.

Before I go into the main problem, I would like to say what I mean by psychotic. I mean that the child's neurotic defences are either insufficient or that the child never reached a stage of emotional development at which neurotic defences could be brought effectively into play. This means to say that the child has been under threat of such conditions as disintegration or lack of contact with reality or depersonalization. Either one gets breakdowns of the kinds that are indicated by these words or else one gets a defensive organization such as a heavily organised withdrawal, the energy for which could not have simply come from ordinary neurotic anxiety. In effect the true self is hidden right away and only emerges under very special conditions if at all. In this defence the patient turns himself into a mental hospital and the true self is a patient hidden away in the back somewhere in a padded cell.

Now in regard to the main point, when you say that psychotics are testable, I think you are talking about adults and the psychotic children who are often quite brilliant in a scattered way. It must be remembered, however, that the total mental hospital population must be taken into consideration if one is to apply what one knows of adults to children. If you were to go into a mental hospital and start testing a seriously withdrawn or disintegrated or depersonalised patient there, you would not have any luck. Is this not true? If you had the good fortune to make a contact you might get very good results on test, but you could not do a test in the state in which they are over long periods. According to my view exactly these same states are common in childhood and the children are very difficult to test when they are in such states. Nevertheless there is a greater possibility in childhood of creating the conditions in which the self can be let out of the padded cell for a time. In my experience these psychotic children that I am talking about come off very badly when tested by the wrong kind of educational psychologist; in fact they always come out as hopelessly defective.

This child H was very obviously an intelligent child until a certain date and then she became a mentally defective child. It might be taken that she had an encephalitis or a brain tumour but there is no evidence of this and in fact in the course of the twice-a-week treatment that J has been able to give there has emerged a completely different child out of the defective condition of a year or two ago.

I very much hope that you will use this case after testing H for a discussion of this very problem. I will try to organise this discussion and I will ask you to come to a little group at this house, probably on the fourth Thursday evening in November, and I will ask J to come as well. I look forward to this.

> Every good wish,
> Yours,
> D. W. Winnicott.

1. The problem was whether psychotic children became more accessible to testing over time, rather than sometimes testable and other times not.

50 ❧ To the Editor, the Times

1st November 1954

Sir,

These has been a report in the press of a magistrate's criticism of an approved school, and if this report is correct it calls for comment. The management of antisocial children is so difficult that those who undertake this work cannot be expected to do their best if the nature of their work is not understood by the public and by the magistrates of juvenile courts.

It appears that Mr. H. R. Dunnico is disturbed to find pin-up pictures on dormitory walls and he looks for an atmosphere in which children spring to attention and say "sir." It may be of course that the approved school in question is a bad one, but the details mentioned in the report of Mr. Dunnico's comment give no indication of this. Can it be said that the real nature of the task of the approved school is not understood by the magistrate?

The issue can be clarified by the sub-division of the problem in the following way. First there is the prevention of delinquency by all sorts of measures, such as adequate housing conditions, full employment, etc., and by education. Secondly there are the very large number of children with antisocial tendencies who do not come before the courts because in some way or other they are helped through a difficult period by the home and by various agencies who give assistance. Thirdly, there are the children whose environment cannot contain their antisocial behaviour and the court steps in to represent the public. In regard to these last children, who have met with public disapproval, the first task of the magistrate is clearly to give proper expression to public reaction so that in the long run the public feels avenged. It is generally understood, however, that no good result can come from revenge, and the second task of the magistrate is to find a way of dealing with the child which protects the offender from the crude expression of public anger. The public expects this and hopes to find that in fact the offender is treated as a human being who has a problem and who suffers.

Those who care for the antisocial boy and girl can do no good whatever if they are motivated by public revenge or by what Mr. Dunnico calls "the idea of instilling discipline, respect and a social conscience." It ought to be known by now that these three things cannot be instilled. The staff of the approved schools know that although they must fail with a certain number of cases in their care, they can succeed with others in so far as they think of them as human beings with a significant past history and with present needs that are fundamentally the same as those of ordinary boys and girls who do not happen to have been thrown over into antisocial behaviour by environmental breakdown. It will be noted that Mr. Dunnico, as reported, makes no mention whatever of the successes or failures of the particular approved school in its task of managing very difficult children and of producing out of the total a certain proportion of real human beings able to take their part in the world. Apparently he is not concerned with such matters. He is concerned, according to the press reports, with the revenge aspect of the public attitude. Does he perhaps not know that people in general, while needing to be avenged, do also need that the actual boys and girls who have got into trouble shall be helped? It is becoming increasingly possible to help some of these unhappy children, but those who do this difficult work can only do well if they are trusted to find their own way of getting to the heart of the matter in each individual case.

Yours etc.
D. W. Winnicott.

51 ⮞ *To Roger Money-Kyrle*

10th February 1955

Dear Money-Kyrle:

There are several reasons why I want to meet yourself and some or all of those I mentioned. Roughly speaking these are:

1. If we meet personally we have no difficulty whatever in be-lieving in each other, and in that case if we happen to disagree on a point or two it does not matter. If we never meet, however, the disagreements get an importance that is out of proportion. Simply meeting and talking about the weather or something is a good thing in itself. We shall never meet, however, unless we organize a meeting.

2. There is the flutter caused by the discussion on K and this should be got out of the way, because the problems that I have in my mind for discussion have nothing to do with K and ante-date him by several years. It is useful to get this stated.

3. The problem of groups within the Society is a very interest-ing one which can be discussed constructively. It is a problem, however, which cannot be left to look after itself. If groups form they must be prepared to state clearly their aims and be prepared also to discuss the effect of the existence of groups on the Society. We can assume, I think, that the main identification of each one of us is with the Society and not with any group. Without the Soci-ety the groups would have no meaning and no power. As Mem-bers of the Society therefore we are interested in the effect of groups. I would like to have the opportunity to put forward for discussion the simple idea that a group in a society is disruptive of the society. This would take about three minutes to state.

4. There is a further point which concerns my interest in the work of Melanie Klein. I would like a further three minutes to put forward for discussion the simple view that the acceptance of Mrs. Klein's work is being seriously held up by propaganda in its fa-vour, and that I personally am alarmed by signs of development on the propaganda side. It has been rather strange to me to see the sponsoring of Melanie Klein's views gradually taken over by a group of analysts. This is a statement that could be discussed and perhaps refuted. Again I would say that what cannot happen is that it should be left in the air.

From my point of view this meeting would not be one that I would talk about, and I would make this clear since any expression of views and feelings would be sealed off in the discussion situation.

Yours,

52 ᴅ᷿ *To Roger Money-Kyrle*

17th March 1955.

Dear Money-Kyrle,

This letter is a wee note about what you said outside the clinic last night. I look forward to the paper in which you bring in the idea of the infant creating the world. I am only writing to ask you to consider my view, which is that it has been very difficult to get Klein followers to see this idea during the past decade. If one mentions it one was considered to be throwing away the whole depressive position concept. Now it seems that it is de rigeur and I think that now it may be possible for members of the Klein group to do the analysis of artists and of artistic productions in ordinary patients.

In my view Adrian Stokes' book[1] is a sad example of an artist who struggles to cram artistic production into the introjection-projection systems and the concept of the depressive position, but the main thing that is evident is his failure since as a creative person he cannot allow it.

With good wishes,
Yours,
D. W. Winnicott.

1. *Smooth and Rough.*

53 ❧ *To Emilio Rodrigue*

17th March 1955

Dear Dr. Rodrigue:

I think that you must feel that your lecture produced an interesting discussion and was much appreciated, especially on account of the bit of clinical material from child analysis. I repeat that it was a great pleasure to have you here in England once more.

I am writing about the little detail which in essence is not the subject of your paper but which arose out of it. In reply to my direct question, you said yes, each infant does create the world. The other half of your sentence I think wants a tail to it, and if you could provide this tail you would then be saying something which is absolutely in line with the sort of thing which I keep on saying over and over again because I think it needs saying. You went on with some words like these: "But the world the infant creates is a chaotic one" (you may not have used the word chaotic but I think you will remember). I am suggesting that here you are brought right up against the mother's presentation of the world to the child and the infant's very great dependence on the mother on this account. If the mother presents the world to the infant in a chaotic way then, as you say, the infant creates a chaotic world. Ordinarily, however, the mother does not present a chaotic world but takes great care even although she is quite uninstructed to simplify the world in such a way that in fact the infant creates a world that increases in complexity in an orderly way. If you could add this tail-piece to what you said it would be very important and it would be in advance of the ordinary Kleinian statement of infancy.

This is a matter of great practical importance not only in the application of psycho-analytic work to mothercraft but also in the analysis of artists and of the artistic efforts of patients.

Talking in the same terms the thing that makes your presentation so interesting, whereas some presentations are dull is that one feels that when you give Klein theories you not only discover them but you also invented them (or created, one could say). It is because of this latter element in your work also that you are likely to do original work as well as presenting Mrs. Klein's and Freud's work in a fresh way.

Please give my very good wishes to your wife and in case I do not see you again before you go back, I wish you all the best.

Yours sincerely,
D. W. Winnicott.

54 ❧ To Charles F. Rycroft

21st April 1955.

Dear Rycroft,

I hope your paper went well last night. I was very grieved to be unable to make it but I have had a rotten cold with sinuses and when I finished work I just found I could not do any more and I went to sleep. I would rather have missed almost any paper than yours, which was very interesting and which deals with a subject which interests me very much, as you know, and which I find difficult to grasp in the sort of way that you seem to be able to do. It is quite one thing to come at a problem through clinical work and to formulate something in one's own language, and another thing to take ideas and interrelate them, thus contributing to the building of theory.

I shall be hearing how the evening went, but I thought I would like you to know why I was not there. Perhaps Marion Milner told you that I was not really well, as she knew about this Wednesday middle day.

Yours,
D. W. Winnicott.

55 ❧ To Michael Fordham

26th September 1955

My dear Fordham:

Thank you for your letter. I don't want to stop our correspondence at this point. Please try to find time to answer this second letter.

Firstly, you have not dealt with my main point, perhaps because I introduced other ideas. Can you answer it now? Do you see what I mean and do you agree? There are two points of view, and when I say the environment must have a theoretical start of absolute adaptation I am only talking of one point of view: that of the observer. The infant is not yet emerged from primary identification. (We are referring to processes that belong chiefly to the very start—i.e. even before birth.)

Secondly, don't you agree that when we use the word self, a perfectly good English word, we are agreed about the term, even although we may differ as to what we can use it for in our descriptions of any one stage of an individual's development; by contrast, when we use the term Ego we are introducing a term for our own benefit, and we must define it. I think Freud started off this idea of using the term Ego and we are therefore bound to follow his developments in the use of the term, and justify our variations in the use of the term. I think that Jung did a disservice to clear thinking by distorting Freud's term, Ego, and thus making it very difficult to follow the developing ideas of the way the term can be useful.

The term conscious presents a special difficulty. You use the word as a term when a perfectly good English word "self-conscious" is at hand. I don't believe Jung intended this muddle, it is a matter of translation, and I wish you could put it right. It's all difficult enough anyway, especially for intelligent young students coming at psychology and making a genuine attempt to assess each contributor's contribution.

We seem to agree that another language will have to be used to clear up the mess, but we ought all of us (I'm no angel) to avoid using ordinary English words as terms, and avoid failing to use ordinary English words when they are available.

At any rate try to write me about my first point.

Yours ever,
D. W. Winnicott

Winnicott around 1935.

At a conference in 1963.

With Anna Freud at the banquet to mark the completion of the Standard Edition of the Works of Freud, 1966.

In the Buckingham Palace studio of Oscar Nemon. Winnicott led a fund drive to have Nemon's statue of Freud (at upper right) cast in bronze and erected in London. The statue now stands in Swiss Cottage. Winnicott liked to stroll down to Nemon's studio on Saturday mornings and make forms out of plaster himself. Nemon's bust of Winnicott is on display in the offices of the British Psycho-Analytical Society.

A portrait by Lotte Meitner-Graf, published with Winnicott's obituary in the *British Journal of Medical Psychology* in 1971.

Winnicott enjoyed sketching and could capture a mood, a set of shapes, a relationship with just a few lines.

Winnicott in 1970.

56 ❧ To Hanna Segal

6th October 1955.

Dear Dr. Segal:

While we were talking last night I was particularly interested in your talking about a third area of operation in the communication between analyst and patient. I expect I have got the wording wrong but you will remember the part that I am referring to. You can imagine that I find it rather exciting to watch this idea being developed out of clinical material. I think that there is a very great deal to be got out of the study of what you were talking about and I hope that you will make a special point of developing what you were talking about into a paper. You know, of course, that I am interested in this because of my own attempt represented in the paper Transitional Phenomena etc.

Another thing about what you said was that it continued the theme of the essential difficulty of communication which belongs to the psychotic and which I suppose lies at the basis of a great deal of psychotic illness. I am sorry to say that Bion slurred over this point but he had plenty of other things to talk about so that we can forgive him.

Don't bother to answer.

Yours,
D. W. Winnicott.

57 ❧ To Wilfred R. Bion

7th October 1955.

Dear Bion,

I find I want to write to you about your Wednesday paper.[1] First I would like to say that I think of you as the big man of the future in the British Psycho-Analytical Society. You have a strong personality and there could be a danger that you would get into the forefront by this means instead of by the natural development of circumstances. I am sure you would not like this to happen. The strength of your personality makes it difficult for people to get up and tell you that you are in a muddle or that you have said something wrong, and at the meeting on Wednesday your relation to the Society was completely spoiled by the fact that the first three or four speakers were Mrs. Klein and the pro-Kleinians. The impression was given that you were being protected from the Society and I really believe you must hate this sort of thing, as you are quite capable of defending yourself and of enjoying a contact with people who feel they want to challenge something you have said. After you had been insulated from the Society by the first four speakers there was no hope whatever that someone would get up and challenge you. This is a matter of procedure which wants seriously looking into, and I have tried very hard to get into contact with the Klein group in order to point out to them the harm that they are doing to the Klein cause by this sort of behaviour.

In 10 years' time I believe that you will find yourself in contact with the whole Society but you have not yet started, being as you are cluttered round by the organisation of the Kleinian group. I find myself able to vituperate against the Klein group without in the least altering my view of Mrs. Klein as a loveable person to whom I owe as much as I do to Freud and who has contributed so very fully on the scientific side. Mrs. Klein seems to be unable to see, however, that her followers are disrupting the Society since they stand together in a block and there is no entry into this block except by the process of being analysed by Mrs. Klein or by someone analysed by her and so on.

As I hope that you will be President soon, I very much want to feel I have expressed my point of view clearly because you cannot emerge as President of the whole Society until you have emerged from the Klein grouping. I hope you will see that this has nothing to do with the adherence to the scientific truth unveiled by Mrs. Klein and to the line of investigation set going by her own discoveries. It has to do with group behavior in relation to the Society.

Your paper contained a great deal more than anyone in the room was able to assimilate. As a matter of fact I think you did not read it very well and so therefore you did yourself some injustice . . . it was a challenging and difficult paper. There are many things about it that gave me pleasure, especially your attempt to describe a part of a session, and I think that you did this more convincingly than has been achieved for a long time in the Society. One felt convinced that you were making a completely honest attempt to report what had happened even if you found yourself disagreeing (as you pointed out) with an interpretation given. I feel very much in sympathy with your idea that your interpretation was probably the right one at the moment even if after it is given it immediately becomes inadequate or inaccurate.

I would like to go a little further in expressing what I started to speak to you about when I took part in the discussion. It does seem to me that the material that you reported cried out for an interpretation about communication.

It is true that the interpretations you made were very likely right at the moment but if one violates the reported scene by taking it in abstract, always a dangerous thing to do, I would say that if a patient of mine lay on the couch moving to and fro in the way your patient did and then said: "I ought to have telephoned my mother" I would know that he was talking about communication and his incapacity for making communication. Should it interest you to know, I will say what I would have interpreted: I would have said: "A mother properly oriented to her baby would know from your movements what you need. There would be a communication because of this knowledge which belongs to her devotion and she would do something which would show that the communication had taken place. I am not sensitive enough or orientated in that way to be able to act well enough and therefore I in this present analyic situation fall into the category of the mother who failed to make communication possible. In the present relationship therefore there is given a sample of the original failure from the environment which contributed to your difficulty in communication. Of course you could always cry and so draw attention to need. In the same way you could telephone your mother and get a reply but this represents a failure of the more subtle communication which is the only basis for communication that does not violate the fact of the essential isolation of each individual."

You will see that from my point of view you were talking about the environment although you said you were not going to do so and you were indicating by this clinical material that this man has a relative lack of capacity for communicating because of some experiences in which his mother or whoever was there failed in the original maternal task at the stage when the mother is closely identified with her baby, i.e. at the very beginning.

I know that there is a tremendous amount other than this sort of thing in the psychotic illness and that all the other things that you and others bring in are important, notably the parking out of personal elements in the environment. You happen to give clinical material, however, which screamed out for an interpretation about communication and this is why I want to make this comment.

As a subsidiary point, one which leaves this interesting scientific consideration and goes back to group behavior, I do feel that the Society gets awfully bored with the plugging of terms. In the last six months the words "projective identification" have been used several hundred times. Of course we are in for a few months in which the word "envy" will be brought in everywhere. As you know, the words "internal objects" came across in every communication right up to the time when projective identification took their place. There is something wrong here and I believe and hope that you will take part in the attempt we must make if the Society is to survive to get behind these disruptive tendencies, which are of the nature of a plugging of theme-songs. Incidentally, I am very doubtful about the value of the words "projective identification" when applied to the parking out of the minute particles of the personality since the word identification rather implies a whole human being somewhere. I would have thought that nearly the whole development of the projective identification theory was contained in the ordinary analytic theory of paranoid anxiety, but perhaps you can put me right here if I am wrong.

I realise that this is a very long letter and that you are a very busy person. I am sorry that in this letter I have had to deal with two completely different themes, one of them intensely interesting, which is the scientific discussion of clinical material of psychotics, and the other the irritating theme of group behaviour. I would not like to write you two letters, however, at the same moment, and I have taken the risk of putting everything into one letter.

Incidentally I am very interested in your development of the theme of the neurotic part of the personality which, so to speak, brings the psychotic part to analysis, a theme which interests some of the Americans and which I have referred to in the language of the false self hiding the true self and eventually allowing the true self to emerge for analysis.

I think we have very exciting times in front of us on the scientific side in psycho-analysis. I hope the political scene will not go on spoiling the scientific work.

Good wishes,
Yours,
D. W. Winnicott.

1. "Differentiation of the Psychotic from the Non-psychotic Personalities."

58 ❧ To Anna Freud

18th November 1955.

Dear Miss Freud,

I am trying to put together a small contribution which seems to me to follow your paper Psycho-Analysis and Education and the discussion as reported in Volume 9 of the Psycho-Analytic Study of the Child.

I feel that so many important things were said by you in the course of that discussion that they lead naturally on to a more definite statement than was made of the emotional state of the mother at the very beginning of the infant's existence. This has been referred to but rather in terms of a biological state, and the word symbiosis has been used.

All this ties up very much with the difficulties that the Society is having at the moment in tracing the early roots of unfused aggression, this being reflected in my opinion in Mrs. Klein's temporary (I hope) insistence on what she calls innate envy, something which involves the idea of a variable genetic factor.

I am writing to you because I am wondering whether you have a group that I could write this short paper for so that it could be discussed. I would be quite contented, of course, if you were to say that it would be best if I were to write it and send it to you and have a talk with you about it personally. I somehow feel that, being human, I need an audience of at least one so that I may orientate to the presentation of my idea.

I know how busy you are but I know also that you can defend yourself and I need not mind asking you for this favour.

I would like to say how very much I have enjoyed this contribution of yours in Volume 7 [*sic*] and I want to thank you again for mentioning my name.

Yours very sincerely,
D. W. Winnicott.

59 ❧ To Joan Riviere

3rd February 1956

Dear Mrs. Riviere:

After Mrs. Klein's paper[1] you and she spoke to me and within the framework of friendliness you gave me to understand that both of you are absolutely certain that there is no positive contribution to be made from me to the interesting attempt Melanie is making all the time to state the psychology of the earliest stages. You will agree that you implied that the trouble is that I am unable to recognize that Melanie does say the very things that I am asking her to say. In other words, there is a block in me. This naturally concerns me very deeply and I very much hope you will give me a little bit of your time. I would willingly call on you if you do not feel like writing a letter. Enclosed are the notes from which I chose certain passages when speaking after Melanie's paper.

There is no need for me to try to tell Melanie how to do analysis. If I am any good at analysis myself it is largely due to her work and also to yourself. Also the work Melanie had done recently, drawing our attention to projective identification and now to envy, is undoubtedly valuable, although I would like to say that her contributions in these respects can be overvalued since analysts have surely been using these ideas for a long time. It was useful to be reminded of projective identification. In regard to envy, I think it valuable that Melanie has drawn our attention to the fact that the concept of penis envy, which has come into analysis for years and years, can have roots in breast envy. In other words, when envy turns up in the transference it is not necessary for us to assume that the analyst is in the father role. The question arises, however, when envy turns up and the analyst is in the maternal role, whether it is not better to stick to the idea or potency even though a modified idea of potency must be ascribed when it is of the mother figure that we speak.

Surely Melanie's paper had three themes which were mixed up in a way which made discussion almost impossible. I am surprised to find Melanie writing such a muddled paper. The first theme is the theme of envy as it appears in analysis, and here her contribution is positive and acceptable and valuable, although not new. The second theme is that of the infant's envy of the good breast. Here Melanie is looking at the infant as brought to the analysis by the child or adult patient. The third is her attempt to state the psychology of earliest infancy. In the second I feel that she has raised problems which are by no means solved and in the third I feel that she has let herself down badly by making a statement which it is very easy to pull to pieces, and which can easily hold up the study of the development of Ego stability and the researches which are going on in various parts of the world into the treatment of psychosis. I think it is necessary that Melanie does not deal with psychotic patients although of course she has a vast experience of psychotic material as it appears in patients who are not actually mental hospital material.

It is little wonder that a paper which muddles up these three distinct themes produced a poor discussion. The only thing that can happen is that those who like to support Melanie produce, as we could all do, clinical material or quotations from the Bible which support her theme. Anyone dealing with the other two subjects must be in an odd position because the themes are in odd positions relative to each other.

My trouble when I start to speak to Melanie about her statement of early infancy is that I feel as if I were talking about colour to the colour-blind. She simply says that she has not forgotten the mother and the part the mother plays, but in fact I find that she has shown no evidence of understanding the part the mother plays at the very beginning. I must say this quite boldly in spite of the fact that I have never been a mother and she, of course, has. You, too, have been a mother, and you are entitled to your own opinion about my capacity to deal with these matters. You have expressed to me often that you value my statements of the mother-infant relationship, and I want to ask you whether you could carry the matter a little further and consider whether perhaps there is not something in the theory at this point that I can contribute. If I contribute to psychoanalytic theory it is not of course necessary for me to be accepted by either yourself or Melanie Klein, but I do in fact mind tremendously if I really have a positive contribution to make, however small, and if this cannot find acceptance either with you or with Melanie.

An example of the way in which communication with Melanie is difficult on this point—I would take the matter of her statement to the effect that there is the "good breast" and there is the infant, and the result is an attack on the breast. I know very well indeed that this is true and I know that it is the good breast and not the bad breast that the infant bites. Nevertheless in talking in this way we are leaving out the Ego development of the infant and we are therefore not making a statement of earliest infancy. The "good breast" is not a thing, it is a name given to a technique. It is the name given to the presentation of breast (or bottle) to the infant, a most delicate affair and one which can only be done well enough at the beginning, if the mother is in a most curious state of sensitivity which I for the time-being call the State of Primary Maternal Preoccupation. Unless she can identify very closely with her infant at the beginning, she cannot "have a good breast," because just having the thing means nothing whatever to the infant. This theme can be developed, and I have frequently attempted to develop it, and I shall continue to develop it because I know of its great importance not only to mothers with infants but also to analysts who are dealing with patients who have for a moment or over longer phases been deeply regressed.

It is a matter of great grief to me that I cannot get Melanie to take up this point or to see that there is a point here to be discussed.

You may wonder why I am writing to you and not to Melanie. It would seem likely that Melanie will not want to be bothered with me and my ideas especially in view of the fact that she will not meet any analysts except those who are glad to welcome her contribution in respect of its first theme. I know, however, that you have always been in close touch with Melanie and in any case I have an interest in your opinion of me for obvious reasons. The one thing that would make me doubt about writing to you is the sentence in the preface to the Klein book[2] which you wrote and which you know shocked me, in which you implied that the Klein system of thought had covered everything so that there was nothing left to be done but to widen the application of the theories.

I shall understand if you have too much on hand to be willing to take up this matter with me. I feel, however, that I want you to know that I do not accept what you and Melanie implied, namely that my concern about Melanie's statement of the psychology of earliest infancy is based on subjective rather than objective factors.

Yours sincerely,
D. W. Winnicott

1. "A Study of Envy and Gratitude."
2. See letter to Melanie Klein, 17 November 1952, note 2.

60 ❧ To Enid Balint

22nd March 1956.
Dear Enid:

I want to let you know in a more formal way than I was able to let you know last night that I think your paper[1] is a very good one and that the work on which it is founded is absolutely first-class. I say this even although you feel you took quite a long time getting the feel of the case, as well you might.

I want you to give some thought to the wording of your reference to me, especially if you are thinking of publishing the paper, which I hope you will do. You say on page 11 that I particularly discuss regression to full oral dependence. Probably you will not find that I have used the term oral dependence, and it would seem to me that I have rather specially avoided mixing up two things, i.e. regression to dependence and regression in terms of instinct stages. Regression to dependence, which I have talked rather a lot about, seems to me not to be specifically linked to the oral phase, and indeed I want to cut it loose from the phases and from the instinctual development and allow it therefore to relate to ego relatedness which precedes instinctual experience that is accepted as such.

I expect you see what I mean and the omission of the words "full oral" would clear up the difficulty. I think that I am referring to almost the same thing that Michael [Balint] calls the primary mother.

To repeat myself, I very much enjoyed last night and I was glad, although the discussion was a poor one. It is ever so boring when people get up and use the material you have given to show you how they could have interpreted better. I am afraid I have done quite a lot of this myself in the Society ten or twenty years ago, but it is maddening and has nothing to do with a scientific discussion of the many interesting points raised in your paper.

Every good wish,
Yours,
D. W. Winnicott.

1. "Three Phases of a Transference Neurosis."

61 ᵉᵛ *To Gabriel Casuso*

4th July 1956.

Dear Dr. Casuso:

I was very glad indeed to get your little note about your son.[1] This note is very interesting indeed and shows what a lot there is for us to learn about small children.

I am sure I have no very important comment to make, except to state the obvious. It is interesting that this intellectual interest in the penis turns up in your healthy child at about a year. I think it rather important to separate out the mind here from the psyche-soma. It is not possible to deduce from this very clear observation that the child has no previous trace in the psyche of something which eventually becomes joined on to the idea of a penis. In other words, you are talking about the boy's mind, which had got so far at that point as to be able to think about this special part of himself. Previous to this there had undoubtedly been some phallic sensations, and I think you refer to occasional erections.

It seems to me that the idea of what in psychoanalytic terms is called a penis originally turns up in respect of certain qualities in the mother such as rules and regulations, timing, hardness, indestructability. At a variable date these ideas gather together and may be handed over to the father if he happens to be around.

Here is building up the idea of an indestructable element that easily forms a root for eventual appreciation of a paternal phallus. Before this happens there are several side-tracks, one of which is the idea of a maternal phallus. Alongside these things we get the beginnings of the child's phallic experiences which are very feeble, no doubt, and as you have so interestingly pointed out, there is the intellectual appreciation which helps or hinders according to the infant's experiences and the behaviour of the environment.

What a task the infant has, bringing together these ideas of his own genitality, and the concept of the paternal phallus which is formed from another root in the way I have tried to describe! It seems to me that observations of the paternal phallus sometimes join up with the one and sometimes with the other root.

Incidentally, it rather amuses me to make an exercise by saying "what is the penis symbolical of?" To some extent the penis is symbolical of a snake or of a baby's bottle or of the baby's body as it moved in the womb before the arms and legs became significant and before there were oral and anal zones. I think that in regard to the one way in which the idea of a penis develops where it is gradually constructed out of certain properties of the mother, then we have to think of a very fundamental concept, and have to say that the snake is symbolical of a penis. When we come, however, to the other extreme such as your son's observation of his penis and his mind-work on the subject, then I think we can look at it the other way and talk about the penis as symbolical of other more fundamental objects as, for instance, the tooth-brush or some other toy or, as I have said, of the fish or reptile that is understood because it is like the infant was at the dawn of impulse.

This is all I can say at the moment and I am wondering what you will think of my comments. There is much more to be learned out of your close observation than I have had time yet to assimilate.

I would like to add that I wish I had had a better opportunity of getting to know you and your wife while you were over here. I only hope that you had a rich experience and that you will take our goodwill back to your country.

Yours sincerely,

1. A paper entitled "Anxiety Related to the 'Discovery' of the Penis."

62 ᴇ᷾ To Oliver H. Lowry

5th July 1956.

Dear Dr. Lowry:

It was good of you to write me about the establishment of a Chair in Child Psychiatry.[1] It would seem that you are to have priority. I have been pressing for some time for a Chair of Child Psychiatry in this country and it may interest you to know that I have asked for an "official announcement that there shall be a Chair of Child Psychiatry in 10 years' time." It has not yet been possible to get University or Paediatric acknowledgement of the need for such a Chair.

In the wording of my recommendation in this country, that there should be a Chair of Child Psychiatry in 10 years' time, I have implied, as you see, that there is no-one here who is fit to hold this post. For the same reason I am not able to recommend someone for Washington. If I change my mind on this subject I will let you know, because indeed there are some over here who are developing rapidly.

In my opinion we should ask for a paediatrician who has had a recognised paediatric training to have added a recognised psycho-analytic training. If this issue is raised in this country there will be protests from the Jungians of whom there are a few who are out-standing, and also from some of the eclectics. I think you will agree with me, however, that we must put forward the claim for the psycho-analytic training, which at any rate in this country is very much better than any other comparable training scheme.

It seems to me that it is most important that child psychiatry shall not be a branch of adult psychiatry but of paediatrics, just as I feel that it is important that the Professor should have not only had a psycho-analytic training, but should also have had several years' experience of child analysis.

In making these suggestions I am implying that selection plays a very important part. The selection for paediatrics and also for psycho-analysis should be sufficient. Even so I feel that there are not many who by temperament and personality can properly fill this very important post, whether it be in this country or in U.S.A.

I am implying that I think that the academic psychological qual-ification is not relevant.

You ask me to discuss further aims and long range objectives, and I would very much like to have time for personal conversation on this subject, which is one to which I have given a good deal of thought. It is difficult to get at good samples of one's thoughts when one has been thinking over a subject for many years.

First in regard to psycho-therapy, the reason why I said that the candidate for the Chair should have had several years of practice in child analysis is that I feel that we must not expect or allow the Professor to fill his time with child analyses and the acute prob-lems of management which belong to any active practice. If he were to keep up three analyses and a few short treatments along-side the occasional therapeutic consultation, I think he would have material for teaching without cluttering up his life with clinical burdens.

He would hope to surround himself with psycho-therapists, some of whom need not be qualified medically. Perhaps in your country they need to be, but we find it quite satisfactory over here to have a proportion, not more than 30%, without the medical qualification.

The teaching would have to be done on live material and on the discussion of the cases, chiefly those having psycho-analytic treatment.

What I feel you will gain by having psycho-analysts rather than statisticians or academic psychologists is that the word research will not come to mean vast projects with questionnaires and an army of investigators who do no good. The advances in our subject are being made at the front end of psycho-analytic treatment at the places where treatment tends to fail or tends to need modification or where we discover our relative deficiencies in training because of problems that do not resolve. Further, the Professor being a psycho-analyst will be in favour of the personal analysis of all those who are taking seriously to child psychiatry. I believe this is accepted in your country in a more universal way than it is over here, and that probably your Psychiatric Social Workers and whatever is equivalent to our Child Care Officers will have had personal analyses.

Something like what you are attempting takes place in this country at the Tavistock Clinic, 2 Beaumont Street, London, W. 1, to which I am not attached, but about which I hear a good deal. You could no doubt gain from contact with Dr. John Bowlby who is the senior child psychiatrist at this clinic, where nearly everyone working has had a psycho-analytic training or an analysis by a psycho-analyst.

In regard to your question, can we aim at finding a person who is both the finest practitioner of child psychiatry and at the same time an outstanding investigator?—I am personally in favour of the former and not in favour of a compromise. I think that an experienced child psycho-analyst at the head of a team will be able to keep the research of the team members in channels which are economic and which do not involve futile investigations which as I have said earlier make no difference to the case, and I would add now that by making no difference these investigations do harm. I feel sure that this will be readily accepted by yourself, and I am told that in your country it is recognised that therapeutics is altered and spoiled by non-therapeutic investigation and that an investigation that spoils therapy is bad teaching.

I would certainly need much more opportunity for discussion if I were to make my opinion clear on this point, and indeed some of my views are not fully developed. In any case I have spoken rather dogmatically in order to deal with your letter by letter.

I would like to end by saying that the really difficult task of the child psychiatry Professor will be to coordinate the two halves of paediatrics, the physical and the psychological, yet it seems to me that he must try to do so in spite of the fact that he will be dealing with a dissociation in the community which plays itself out in the muddled management which the child with psycho-somatic illness usually gets. Here again, however, is a very complex subject which cannot be stated in a few words.

I am very glad that you wrote to me about this subject, to which I have done very much less than justice.

Yours sincerely,

1. Dean Lowry had sought Winnicott's recommendations for candidates for the position, as well as his thoughts on long-range objectives for a program in child psychiatry.

63 ❧ To J. P. M. Tizard

23rd October 1956.

Dear Dr. Tizard:

You have asked me to make a statement for discussion relating to the problem,—Should a mother have her baby in hospital or at home?

It would be generally agreed that this is one of those problems which must be approached from several diverse angles; no one answer can be given, and what you have asked me to do is to speak from the point of view of the psychologist.

The psychologist is concerned with the mother as a person and with the baby as a human being starting on the long road of emotional development.

The Mother.

The essential feature from the mother's point of view when she is about to have a baby is that she shall have confidence in a doctor and also in a nurse. The team is not good enough. Confidence here means that she can take it for granted that what is known in medical science will be applied. I am referring particularly to the physical side of midwifery. The best psychology for a prospective mother is confidence on the physical side. So much of psychology can work itself out naturally if the setting is reliable. This does not mean that nothing must ever go wrong, because a mother is quite capable of accepting human fallibility provided she has had time and opportunity to gain faith in the person who is responsible.

These conditions can be fulfilled in a hospital, but in practice they are more likely to be fulfilled when the general practitioner is able to take responsibility. What is obvious in the small town is also true in the large town, although in the latter case the general practitioner's position tends to be weakened by the existence of specialist clinics.

There are prospective mothers who are apprehensive by nature, and who therefore feel more confident in a clinic, always provided that they are treated as persons and that they know the personnel. Every advantage that can be gained from a clinic on the psychological side can be wiped out, however, if the relationships are impersonal, or if the management is mechanical. Prospective mothers prefer to take physical risks rather than get involved in impersonal management. This is why it is impossible to make a ruling, since clinics vary so tremendously in this matter of the personal relationship between the doctor or the nurse and the prospective mother. It is not infrequently a matter of achievement for a mother who has had her first baby in a clinic to graduate to having a baby at home. She finds enormous advantages in the latter arrangement since she can maintain control except in so far as she is in a dependent state because of the actual birth process. She can have her chosen G.P. She may, of course, happen on a dominating midwife, which undoes the good. One fact must be remembered, which is that a mother at this time is in one sense highly dependent, and she is also liable to feel dominated by any other woman who is in charge. A good midwife, however, only dominates in the nursing sense, that is to say, where she is professionally in charge, and she allows the mother to establish her own rights in her own home. It would be a serious loss to the more normal and healthy women should it become impossible for them to have their babies at home.

Fathers come into this argument since they are seriously neglected in most clinics, whereas at home they play their part even although in the matters of expert midwifery the midwife or the G.P. takes over from him. The father also has his special problems at the time, and his difficulties arise out of the fact that he does fundamentally feel responsible for what is going on. On the whole it is probably the men who will be satisfactory fathers who are most in need of being treated sympathetically and with respect at this special time of the birth of the child. Clinics tend to leave the father out.

After the birth of the baby there is a very big difference according to whether the birth has taken place at home or in a clinic. In a clinic the mother is not in charge and from her point of view as an expert in one thing—the introduction of the baby in the world—she is usually exasperated although too frightened to express her dismay. At home, in so far as she is not too feeble from the physical effort of the birth process, she is in charge, and the fact that she needs help physically should not take away from her responsibility for the initiation of feeding. In some clinics, it is true, things are very well arranged, so that the mother has the baby available for feeding according to what she feels that she and the baby will manage well together, but in most busy clinics the mother is caught up in the clinic rules which may easily include the management of all the babies in a separate room. The mother may not even know whether the baby who is crying is hers or belongs to someone else. It is impossible to over-stress the importance of an intimate relationship between the mother and the baby at the beginning, not only because of the happiness of the mother but also because it is through contact with her baby that she develops the relationship to the baby which she needs to have if she is to become a satisfactory mother. It is not just a matter of breast feeding, but a matter of continuity of relationship unbroken from when the baby was inside—or broken only for short periods during the birth process when the mother is not perhaps conscious.

For most mothers this continuity is so important that they would rather have the pains inherent in child-birth than be given twilight sleep if this results in their not absolutely knowing from experience that the baby is the one that came out of their body. It is these very crude realities, which get slurred over in the clinics, which are of extreme importance to mothers, and it is out of these crudities that there becomes established the thing in the mother which makes for good mothering.

In passing, it should be remembered that the mothers are unlikely to complain when leaving a clinic with their babies. They express only gratitude. It is later on when they look back that they find how much they resented the interference with their early coming to terms with their infants.

Young mothers are in the process of growing up. They learn from one pregnancy to another how much they can take for granted and how much they can risk. One pregnancy is not like another to a mother. On the whole through fearing less they get a richer experience with each succeeding pregnancy up to a certain number. The doctors and the nurses are the servants of the mother and father and must try to serve them well, even if at certain moments through specialised knowledge they must take control. In any case the normal birth process is not an illness and it is not an operation and the parents need not be made to feel that they must do as they are told. On the whole it is easier for parents to maintain the position of employer in relation to doctor and nurse when the birth takes place at home than when it takes place in a clinic.

My point of view is derived from several sources. In the psycho-analysis of mothers one does have the opportunity to reach to feelings which are not usually expressed, and psycho-analysis affords an opportunity for research into this as into other matters. My main source of information is the taking of histories from mothers who bring their children to my clinic. Given time, mothers are able to reach back to the feelings that they have forgotten belonging to the time of the birth of the children, and I have been struck by the tremendous richness that comes into the lives of parents through a good management of the birth process, and also of the resentments that belong to impersonal management and interference from the doctors and nurses with the initiation of the infant-mother relationship. This resentment is not usually voiced but it embitters the lives of many women, especially when they can trace difficulties in their children right back to early infancy and to a failure in their earliest relationship which was brought about by the sort of management that is usual in clinics.

The Baby.

It is not necessary to deal with this subject separately under the heading of the baby's needs. The baby's needs can be met both at home and in hospital and they can also be seriously interfered with in either place. The baby needs something at the beginning from the mother which only the mother is in a position to give, and the problems around this have already been discussed. The baby is not sufficiently developed to be able to distinguish between home and hospital, but there is a great difference for the baby between personal and mechanical management from the moment of birth onwards.

Yours sincerely,
D. W. Winnicott.

64 ∾ *To Barbara Lantos*

8th November 1956.

Dear Dr. Lantos,

I am grateful to you for the trouble you took preparing a paper for last night.[1] My respect and affection for yourself does not allow me to pretend that I think this was one of your best contributions. I think you yourself will feel as I do that it would have been better if you had had time to get the paper written down.

In a general way I feel that it is extremely important to get written down the part in which you claim to reproduce the psychoanalytic point of view, which is always a difficult thing to do because of the changes in psycho-analytic theory. Probably no-one was quite satisfied with your presentation of this part of your contribution. I personally was quite bewildered by the tremendous amount you tried to cover, in the centre of which was your very important repudiation of the idea of the infant's aggressive attack on the mother. It would have been important to have had this discussed but alongside it were other contributions such as your interesting theme of primal repression, which Miss Freud picked out.

I think it is not good for the Society to have all these themes in the air with no possibility of having any one of them properly discussed, and I suggest that we must make every effort in our precious scientific meetings to get papers written and circulated at least a week before the meeting. If I had had your paper in time I would certainly have tried to get you to pick out one theme which you could have presented briefly and which could have been fully discussed. When I say this I look back with horror on many evenings when I have read papers to the Society which I had not finished in time to have circulated and which were overloaded with ideas in the same way that I think your paper was last night.

I look forward to a paper from yourself on a concise subject, such as primary repression—a short paper which leaves plenty of time for discussion and which can be thoroughly digested before the actual night on which you read it.

Every good wish,
Yours,

P. S. I find I want to go on writing a little further on the impact of your paper on myself, this time trying to be a bit constructive.

I want to start with the idea primary repression and your assumption that there is something in human beings which belongs to the search for prey and the attack on it. For the time being I will leave out the part which I feel that it is valuable to be reminded of, namely the aggression which is left over when only sublimations or displacements represent, as they must do in the human being, the original impulse. This idea has been put forward by others and by myself in terms of the mother "fobbing off" the child with a feed that is satisfactory. I have even described an infant who seemed to have a fit when fed by a mother whose breasts were so full that enough milk squirted from the breasts into the infant's mouth so that the infant was even robbed of the satisfaction of sucking.

I want to leave this aside for the moment and ask you whether you cannot allow that this which comes in primary repression is exactly what Mrs. Klein and Co. (myself included) are talking about when reference is made to the primitive attack of the infant on the mother's breast? These views do not depend on anything to do with an acceptance of the death instinct and I personally find no value in this part of Freud's theory. Also I agree that the infant does not "want to eat the mother." This is carrying back to the infant language which belongs to a later stage; nevertheless a very important part of our work depends on our finding in our patients the attack on the mother exactly as I have proved over and over again in the way that Melanie Klein describes. I really do feel that what you are saying is that you are unable in your psycho-analytic work to find this early prey-seeking aggression which comes under what you call primary repression. This is not a convincing argument to those who do in fact find it although with great difficulty. There are some things that the Kleinians do in presenting their case which I strongly disapprove of, and perhaps you are confused by these things. For instance, the Kleinians do not seem to allow in their statements for Ego immaturity, so that they seem to ascribe to the newborn infant such things as "baby wanting to eat mother." This is a matter of language to some extent, but tribute should be paid to the fact that Ego development does not admit of such a description of the aim of the small infant. Nevertheless it is necessary to retain the idea of the attack on the mother's body which is ruthless and which only gradually gathers to itself guilt feeling, gradually that is to say as Ego development proceeds.

Another Kleinian mistake seems to me to lie in their attempt to talk about the infant apart from the mother's care of the infant, whereas I believe this to be impossible. I would level this criticism also at many who are outside the Kleinian group. Also there are some who talk only in terms of child care and who forget the infant that has a personal development unless very ill (in which

case there is no more than a collection of reactions to impinge-
ments in spite of physical health).

The fact remains, however, that in psycho-analytic work many
of us using varying techniques recurringly reach the ruthless
primitive love impulse in which the body—breast—mother—or
whatever it is called—undergoes ruthless attack and the result is
something important taken out and eaten, that is to say, destroyed. We do in fact reach in our analyses something which you
say has undergone primary repression, and in saying this you imply that it cannot be reached in analysis. There is a very big difference of opinion here which I think is unnecessary; if only you
could say that in your analyses you do not reach to this although
you do in fact reach very important and deep instinctual impulses
and conflicts.

The main gist of what I am saying in this extra bit tagged on to
my letter is that while saying that Mrs. Klein's finding of the primitive ruthless attack on the mother is not to be found in analysis of
individuals, you are also pointing out that this primitive ruthless
attack is present in human beings as a residue of prey-seeking. The
only difference therefore between the two views is that you hold
that this cannot be reached in analysis and those of us who have
found value in Melanie Klein's work claim that we are sometimes
able to reach this very thing, and that reaching it produces important changes in the patient.

I can see that we could enjoy discussing this point and I only
wish that last night there had been one thing like this that we
could have all discussed.

1. "On the Problem of Aggression."

65 ❧ To Anna M. Kulka

15th January 1957.

Dear Dr. Kulka:

At last I have been able to read your paper "Kinesthetic Needs
and Motility in Earliest Infancy" several times. Naturally you
wished for a comment from me in October. What I want to say

now is more of a general comment of appreciation than a criticism of detail. I find your paper very interesting. Your references to the literature seem to me to be relevant and helpful to those who may want to be led towards the same subject. By the way, have you read the paper—"Importance du rôle de la motricité dans la relation d'objet" (Pierre Marty et Michael Fain), based on a paper read at the Congress of psycho-analysts who speak French and Italian which is held in the autumn in Paris? This paper was given in 1955. I am not sure how far it overlaps with your own work.

Personally I am most interested in the study of the movements in premature infants which give an indication of what happens in the foetal state which indicates life and liveliness. For instance, it has often come my way in an analysis to interpret a snake not as a phallic symbol but as a symbol of the infant's whole self as represented in the body and body movements that are characteristic round the birth date. You seem to me to be dealing with this difficult problem of the infant's task, and therefore the task of those who are caring for the infant, which is to gather up as much as possible of whatever there is of the early vitality into the general service of love and hate. No doubt there is always a certain residue of the earliest activities and muscular urges which is never assimilated to the whole means of expression, and one of the most difficult things I find in analyses is the technique for dealing with unassimilated destructive or aggressive or simply vital urges which turn up clinically in the form of maniacal attacks or more commonly in the form of an inability on the part of the patient to relax. Vigilance has to be maintained against the maniacal episode.

I think that an awfully important part of hypermotility is its relationship to inhibition of oral erotism or, shall I say, the hopelessness about object relationships in oral terms. I think that you bring this point out. It appears in the common statement of parents that the restless child is restless "even at meals." If the mother knew more psychology she would say "especially at meals" because it appears as a substitute for the greedy impulse that can be satisfied.

Certainly we have gone a long way beyond thinking that the infant starts with the oral erotic relationship to the breast and there is a great deal of Ego development prior to the establishment of feeding if this be looked at in terms of an experience of the infant and not simply as a mechanical taking in of food that is offered.

You have probably read the work done on Russian refugees, perhaps by Gorer and I believe others, in which the effect of swaddling on the character was discussed.

I am sending your paper to Dr. Hoffer immediately and I very much hope it will be published in The Psycho-Analytic Study of the Child. I have, of course, no pull in those quarters.

With good wishes and sincere apologies,

D. W. Winnicott.

66   To Thomas Main

25th February 1957.

Dear Dr. Main,

It was natural that at the half-way stage we should have arrived in our discussions at a point where L is under discussion as my special patient. I had to take the opportunity to obtain personal relief after waiting many years before speaking about this case which I believe had in it the possibilities of a clinical result. I am writing to remind you that I am fully aware that this is not the subject which is interesting for you and me to be discussing together; the subject is the type of case, and L certainly falls into the category which you described in your address from the Chair.

In my opinion this work of yours is of importance to psychoanalysis. It may be that psycho-analysis can contribute to your understanding of the problem and that some of the analytic contributions you have not yet absorbed. This is a matter that can be found out. I think that you could be very interested in some of my own work bearing on this subject. It will be fun to try to convey to you the little bit that I think I could contribute as a psycho-analyst. The fact remains, however, that your collecting together of all the fragments of nursing reactions adds up to a real contribution to psycho-analysis.

Roughly speaking I would say that there are two obvious ex-

tremes of people in the world: those who are having psycho-
analysis or could make use of psycho-analysis as we know it, and
by contrast those who have no reason to hope and who therefore
do not worry us. The second category includes a large amount of
the mental hospital population and also a great number of people
living in ordinary society but who have no knowledge that life
could be more satisfactory than it is. I am concerned at the moment about the intermediate area between these two extremes. We
can divide this again into three groups. The first would be those
who have needs derived from early infancy and who just manage
to get through in the course of analysis, partly because they happen to have gone to analysis with an analyst who is willing to
adapt the classical technique where necessary. The third category
in this intermediate area of those who have some hope is largely
made up of those who commit suicide. At the centre is the second
in this category and here we have the kind of patient that you are
describing. The characteristic of this kind of patient is that hope
forces them to bang on to the door of all therapies which might
give the answer. They cannot rest from this and, as you know so
well, their technique for mobilizing activity is terrific in its effi-
ciency. In this particular grouping I think there is a dynamic force
which might destroy psycho-analysis. In practice these patients
could wear down all the available nursing and actual psycho-
analytic personnel. Psycho-analysis cannot ignore this group any
longer but must know that it provides a threat. The psycho-
analyst's life is likely to be threatened by one or two of these patients who always happen to be in his practice, and you hinted of
this in talking of L. Constructive work at the Cassel [Hospital],
you have pointed out, can be disrupted by a few of these patients.

What I am trying to put down in black and white is that these
patients make us try hard because they have hope and because it is
the hope which makes them so clever; yet at the same time the
fact that we cannot provide what is needed produces disaster. In
other words, it is only contributing a little if one can show that
what these patients need is a very complex situation in which they
can regress and in which the psycho-analyst can help them to
make use of a regression. Whatever can be done and is done here
must be only a small bit of what would have to be done to neu-

tralize the destructive potential of this group of people. Indeed I would say that the more psycho-analysts become able to do this kind of work with a few patients the more patients there are who will begin to have hope and therefore will begin to bash around in a ruthless search for a life that feels real. I do consider, therefore, that if psycho-analysts ignore the problem that you have raised in your paper, they are ignoring a group of forces that could destroy psycho-analysis, and in practice could account for the deaths of analysts and psychiatric nursing staff and the breakup of the better type of mental institution.

I think I am only putting into words the sort of things we were saying to each other and I wanted to make quite sure that you knew that I am aware that my very special feeling about L is not the subject under discussion except in so far as my special interest represents an aspect of this general problem.

Yours,

D. W. Winnicott.

67 ❧ *To Melanie Klein*

7th March 1957.

Dear Melanie:

I think everyone enjoyed yesterday evening, including your own contribution.[1]

I am writing about one small detail. I would not like you to think that in asking about the use of the word internal I have forgotten all you taught me twenty years ago. I used the word as Dr. Segal used the word constantly, and I could not be doing my work without always looking for the internal situation as represented in the material of the patient.

May I take it for granted that you know why I asked this question? It is that one half of the Society uses the word internal in this way and the other half does not do so. This is a cause of considerable misunderstanding and it is my job in the Chair to try to give an opportunity for cross fertilization. I may very likely do the same thing again on another occasion or alternatively it may be good to have an evening set apart for the discussion of these terms and their uses.

This matter is of course quite unimportant in relation to Dr. Segal's paper but the same can be said of almost any occasion when the matter arises.

Don't bother to answer this letter. It is only that I wanted to make sure you knew what was going on. As a matter of fact I think Dr. Segal at short notice was not able to give a good account of herself in regard to the use of the word internal, because if you eat your mother up you haven't got a mother inside you. If she had had more time she probably would have distinguished between incorporating and magical introjection, which is what she meant, I suppose.

> Every good wish,
> Yours,

1. Hanna Segal had read a paper entitled "Report on the Analysis of a Man of Seventy-Four," and Melanie Klein had contributed to the discussion.

68 ❧ *To Martin James*

17th April 1957.

Dear Dr. Martin James,

I am glad to hear from anyone staying in Wadebridge. Clare and I will be going to Plymouth on Saturday and I may follow your example and start bathing. Good wishes to you both.

In regard to your letter, I am very glad that you find my paper useful. It does not matter at all if you agree or do not agree with all the details, and I shall hope to learn something from seeing your lectures if you let me have them sometime or other.

The point you make is an interesting one but it seems to me that we are trying to say the same thing. You said disillusionment is a rotten outcome, etc.—happiness is when your illusions come true, etc. I do think, however, that it does fall to the lot of the mother to introduce to the child the facts of external reality. It is for the child to build up a cultural life out of the retention of illusion. I must say I find it all rather difficult but I think this is a good way in, as you suggest, to the discussion of many actual problems of childhood and adult life.

All the best,
Yours,

69 ❧ To Augusta Bonnard

1st October 1957.
Dear Dr. Bonnard:

I am grateful to you for writing me about your proposed paper and its contents. I am glad you enjoyed your travel round the States, and that you survived your friends' hospitality.

In regard to my being the father of the mother, as you put it, I have no idea whatever. I think it very interesting when different observers come to similar conclusions, because it probably means then that they are objectively concerned with real things. For me it is of no importance whatever whether I said something first or whether it was first said by Spitz.[1] What I said came as a natural development of my own way of approaching these matters. You can find traces of everything I have written later in things that I have written earlier, and I suppose it might be rather fun to go into these details, and if I liked I could claim that Dr. Spitz read something of mine ten years ago or that I read something of his at about the same time. I hope that you will simply not care two hoots who was the father and who step-father.

I think that you might be interested in a paper of mine on Maternal Preoccupation. I will enclose a copy along with this but in a month or two my Collected Papers (doesn't that sound grand!) will be really on the market as we have now finished the index, and at the end of this book you will find this paper on Primary Maternal Preoccupation.

I really quite liked your paragraph about these matters, which seems to me to be genuine Augusta Bonnard, influenced perhaps by Spitz and Winnicott, but probably something you would have said yourself anyway apart from us and from Hartmann, so let's enjoy being ourselves and enjoy seeing what we do when we meet it in the works of others. I look forward to your paper.

Yours very sincerely,

1. René Spitz, a leading psychoanalytic experimenter and theoretician in early child development.

70 ❧ To Augusta Bonnard

7th November 1957.

Dear Dr. Bonnard,

I want to let you know in writing as well as in the words that I used yesterday that I very much liked your paper.[1] I think it was rather overloaded, and in fact on second thought I believe that the emphasis on the tongue should have been left for another paper as it sidetracked the main issue. Perhaps you will not agree here but we could have had a better discussion if the paper had been shorter, in which case you would have had to have given us two papers at least.

The main thing is that what you are working at here is something that I find myself deeply in sympathy with. I think that in certain types of case we all of us have wasted a great deal of time interpreting quite correctly on levels which were not the deepest so that the material and the interpretations in the whole analysis are exploited inevitably by the patient who of course would much prefer it if we could get through to the deeper elements.

Very many thanks,
Yours sincerely,

1. "Pre Body-Ego Types of (Pathological) Mental Functioning."

71 ᔰ *To Joan Riviere*

13th June 1958.

Dear Mrs. Riviere,

I would like you to have a note from me before I go to Portugal for a week. You were very kind to me about helping over the Jones obituary.[1]

Naturally I am disturbed that you are upset in regard to the other arrangements.[2] In my opinion what I have done wrong is very slight and ought not to cause any upset. Anyone ringing you up at the present time about a birthday on 28th June must be barmy and I cannot hold myself responsible for such a person. It is true that the notices went out rather early but I had to do something before going away.

I said that I would let you know before doing anything but by this I meant arranging a celebration or writing a notice; in fact you knew about the party as it was all fixed up by Paula Heimann and I was very glad about it. Many other people will be glad too. What I did in sending out the notices did not seem to call for a consultation with yourself.

For some reason or other you are, I think, unduly sensitive about this matter of your birthday. If you just leave it you will find that it works out all right. Those who like to be reminded what an important part you played in the history of the Society or who are fond of you will like to have this opportunity to pay their respects, and the others can ignore the date.

I would like to say something more, which is that there are a lot of generous people in the world, but very few who can receive. I do hope that you will be able on this occasion of your birthday to just receive. Some of what you get will be good, even if the rest is false.[3]

Thank you for the notes about Jones.

Good wishes,
Yours,

1. The obituary was published in the *International Journal of Psycho-Analysis*, 1958.
2. Mrs. Riviere had sent a scathing letter about Winnicott's having notified people about her birthday.

3. This paragraph would seem to enlarge upon what Winnicott said in his 1954 letter to Klein when he complained that Klein had not met his gesture (i.e. his paper). "It was just exactly here that [Mrs. Riviere] failed me."

72 ≈ To R. D. Laing

18th July 1958.

Dear Dr. Laing,

Yesterday I had my first chance to read your MS,[1] which I insulted by getting through it in two hours. You will understand from this that I did not do it justice. After reading it I tried to ring you up because I was so excited. I suppose my excitement had to do with the fact that you make so much use of the sort of things that I think important. Certainly you are very generous in your attributions.

It is possible that in your build-up at the beginning you are talking to yourself quite a bit. This may be a good way of starting a book but I did not really get interested until I was about a third of the way through. I hope the book gets published soon and that from there you may get on to making a more concise theoretical statement.

Incidentally I learned something from your book which is always exciting; something you said about being watched in paranoid states made me see that one of my patients is being watched by a projection of her true self. This is something I had not thought of and it helps me very considerably.

Thank you very much for letting me see the MS. I look forward to reading the book.

Yours sincerely,

1. Laing had sent Winnicott the manuscript of *The Divided Self.*

73 ⅍ *To Herbert Rosenfeld*

16th October 1958.

Dear Dr. Rosenfeld,

I feel like writing to thank you for your paper and for the way you dealt with the questions raised. I agree with Dr. Gillespie that it is very important that this subject should be studied as a subject and not just referred to as it has been in a casual way in the description of cases.

The clinical material in your case rang almost too many bells and I suppose everyone felt that you were talking about the sort of things that happen in their analytic work almost daily and giving some guidance as to how one can best proceed. It amused me when my first case this morning started up with the following remark: "Yesterday I left you thinking that you were going to have a coronary thrombosis, but you are alive; today I am the one just about to die that way." He is a man in whom hypochondriacal symptoms play a large part.

I was not altered by what happened in the discussion in regard to my feelings about the word envy, which I still think adds nothing whatever to the full meaning of oral sadism and which I think introduces the complication of a serious nature, making communication between Kleinians and non-Kleinians very difficult. You will probably agree that it is very important that this matter should be thoroughly thrashed out.

Thanking you again,
Yours very sincerely,

74 ⅍ *To Victor Smirnoff*

19th November 1958.

Dear Dr. Smirnoff,

Thank you for your further letter about the translation into French of Transitional Objects and Transitional Phenomena. I will try to help you over the points you raise.

Page 1, col. 2, line 12.
affectionate type of relationship.
The word "affectionate" in English means something very like the word "tender" but it is not used in just the same places. There is a display of an affectionate relationship when two people who are in love with each other touch with their hands and tingle. Undoubtedly instinct is implied but it is not at the same time operative. If you watch a small child you sometimes see an erotic type of relationship between the child's thumb and the mouth and at the same time an affectionate relationship between the fingers and the area of the upper lip and nose. It is the affectionate type of relationship which is typically lost in the delinquent or even in the early stages of delinquency. Perhaps there is no word in your language which just expresses all this which is sublimated affect and which is very characteristic of most of what a normal child displays in the way of feeling.

The word "tender" is rather good but it emphasizes an absence of aggression and destruction whereas the word "affectionate" neither emphasizes or denies it. One could imagine a hug, for instance, being affectionate and yet far from tender.

Page 2, col. 1, line 5.
imaginative elaboration of function etc.
I will try to explain what I mean by this whole paragraph. Let us assume that someone is trying to make a comprehensive brief statement of human nature. He might do this referring to the individual's pattern of external relationships. He might, on the other hand, do this same thing in terms of the patient's relationship to his inner psychic reality. Usually the attempt is made to relate the one to the other and it is sometimes implied that human nature consists in a mixture of these two aspects each of which enriches the other. In making this statement account is necessarily taken of fantasy, conscious and unconscious, fantasy about external matters and the more mystical psychic phenomena also. In psychoanalytic theory it is generally taken for granted that the ego is a body ego, that is to say, the whole structure of the personality is built up on body functioning and the fantasy that accompanies body functioning. I have used the term imaginative elaboration of

function to describe this theory of the fantasy and psychic reality as being at its origin an elaboration of function. An example of function would be putting the thumb in the mouth. For the human infant, however, this function is elaborated. It is never so simple as that. It means being in control of the thumb which stands for all other objects which are gathered together in this way and put into relationship with the mouth, etc. etc. In other words, function has a meaning for the individual, at first very simple but later highly complex. I wonder if you can get from this some idea of my meaning.

I am laying the ground in this first paragraph for the next paragraph in which I say that a comprehensive statement of human nature must include a third intermediate area of experiencing. This is the area which I associate with the Transitional Phenomena and Objects.

Page 2, col. 2 (4) (bottom of page).
mouthing

By mouthing I simply mean manipulating with the mouth. The baby can be said to put the thumb in the mouth as if this were an experience of the thumb. One can look at it the other way round, however, as an experience of the mouth and then mouthing means what the mouth does to the thumb. It does not necessarily imply the production of sounds but it implies a relationship with an object via the mouth.

Page 3, col. 2 (7)
go inside

I like the rather awkward literal French translation because the word 'introject' implies an intellectual process rather than a matter of the psyche-soma. I think you may find a tendency for the French language to take you over into the intellectual concept and away from the psyche-soma or the rather literal meaning of the words inside and outside, which are more appropriate I feel when we are talking about early infancy. The position of the thumb, for instance, neither inside nor outside is probably important to the infant at the time of birth when there is not much intellect available for introjection and projection mechanisms. Nevertheless I recognise that in translating you may decide to use the word 'introjection,' which would be correct except for the objections that I have raised, that the mechanism is crude and almost physical.

Page 4, col. 2, line 14.
comforter

A comforter in this context means something that comforts. It is not a piece of rubber. Comfort implies the recognition that there is trouble.

Page 5, in the comparative study.
cult.

This word 'cult' is difficult for you to translate because it is not very well chosen. It was the word given by the parent and it seemed to fit at the time. The child collected objects because of certain similarities and sorted them because of certain dissimilarities. I think that your term might be used, 'un veritable cult.' An alternative English word would be 'a collection of objects.'

Page 6, col. 1, line 15.
deadness

Deadness here means simply lack of aliveness and of all the features which characterise the state of being alive.

Page 6, col. 2, line 15.
maternal failure.

Failure here is an equivalent for insufficiency.

Page 6, footnote 11, col. 2.
resting place of illusion.

This is certainly rather a curious way of putting things. I mean that there is a constant struggle in the individual throughout life, distinguishing fact from fantasy, external from psychic reality, the world from the dream. The Transitional Phenomena belong to an intermediate area which I am calling a resting place because living in this area the individual is at rest from the task of distinguishing fact from fantasy.

Page 8, subtitle.
disillusionment.

Yes, there is a reason why I use 'disillusionment.' I think there is no English noun disillusion although there is the verb.

Page 8, col. 2, line 24.
delusion.

Yes, I do mean delusion here in the hallucinatory sense although not necessarily a visual hallucination; it could be a belief.

Page 9, col. 1, line 14.
basis of initiation of experience.

Here I am trying in my summary to relate experiencing to the transitional phenomena.

I am implying that actual experiencing does not stem directly either from the individual's psychic reality nor from the individual's external relationships. This sounds rather startling but you can perhaps get my meaning if you think of a Van Gogh experiencing, that is to say, feeling real, when painting one of his pictures, but feeling unreal in his relationships with external reality and in his private withdrawn inner life. I think that this idea badly needs working out but it is this sort of thing that I am trying to convey that is giving you trouble here.

Let me know if there are any other points or if some of this is still obscure.

Many thanks.
Yours sincerely,
D. W. Winnicott.

75 ⮞ *To Donald Meltzer*

21st May 1959.
Dear Dr. Meltzer:

I think you must have felt that your paper[1] was enjoyed last night. Personally I am glad you read it slowly, although it meant that you took about fifty minutes instead of twenty. It would not have been an easy paper for people to discuss unless they had had the material in front of their eyes, and even this they would want to study well before getting further than an understanding of the material.

I think you will agree with me that it is only possible to make long interpretations like the ones that you reported under special circumstances and when the patient has a high I.Q. It is unfortunate that the sort of presentation which you gave last night makes people feel that the followers of Mrs. Klein talk more than their patients do. Perhaps they do speak more than other analysts, and I would very much like to know about this. In a report of a case, however, if the analyst makes too long an interpretation, the listener gets the impression that the analyst is talking to himself rather than to the patient.

You will understand that I have no doubt at all about the significant bit of work which you reported, and I personally value the opportunity for examining what you did and trying to learn from it. My general comments have to do with my wish that those who report work such as yours could do so in a way which would be acceptable to the Society as a whole, and you will have realised that last night's meeting was defective in one special respect, which was that one-third of the Society was not present. My personal opinion is that B.-groupers[2] stay away from these meetings because if they come they are listening to a language which is foreign to them, and they find this boring. One day you will be able to state what you were doing in a language which will be understandable by the whole Society.

May I repeat to you that I wish to thank you and congratulate you.

Yours sincerely,
D. W. Winnicott.

1. "Notes on a Transient Inhibition of Chewing."
2. Members and students led by Anna Freud.

76 ᙭ *To Elliot Jaques*

13th October 1959.
Dear Dr. Jaques,

I feel like writing to you about your paper[1] because I may have failed to convey to you that I found it to be a valuable contribution in spite of the fact that I questioned your statement about psychoanalysis being the most difficult kind of work (or something of that kind of thing). I really am very interested in the development of your theme and I hope that you will yourself continue to write along the same lines. For instance, I would like to hear your comment on the difference between the work of a student and the work of someone who is in a job. I think you will easily know what I mean in that I am referring to the case of the eternal student who is able to work very hard indeed but only on condition that it is not a job.

I know that I speak in rather a flippant way at times, but I was really quite serious about the difference between doing an analysis and writing a paper. The kind of analysis that I do is carried along by the patient, not by me, whereas a paper is obviously not the same in this respect. I could have said that a paper that one is writing never turns round and says: "Hi! wake up!" Could it be that there are some people who do analyses in a more active way than I do and who do not lean on a process in the patient so that the analysis rests on the basis of work done by the analyst? I do not think really that this was what you were intending to convey. This is a point that the Society is very much interested in.

I hope you will gather from this letter that I am really very interested in your statement and I am looking forward to other papers from yourself on the same sort of subject.

With good wishes,
Yours sincerely,

1. "Disturbances on the Capacity to Work."

77 ᨆ *To Thomas Szasz*

19th November 1959.

Dear Dr. Szasz,

I am writing to you about the questionnaire which you kindly sent me.[1] I know that you are a very serious worker in the field of research as well as being a psycho-analytic colleague. I hope you will not mind that I have decided not to fill in this questionnaire. In my opinion it is not a good questionnaire. There is no way of filling it in which would give an accurate picture of my practice or of my views as an analyst or a child psychiatrist.

I hold the opinion that this sort of questionnaire is dangerous because the definite answers expressed in numerical form will lead to the drawing of certain conclusions and I believe that no such conclusions can be drawn because of the fact that no-one's views or practice can be represented in this way.

I could give detailed criticisms but I am simply writing here to say that in my opinion I would be taking part in something false if I were to send in a filled-up form.

With good wishes,
Yours sincerely,

1. The questionnaire asked for data about practice and a range of the analyst's beliefs.

78 ❧ *To Michael Balint*

5th February 1960.

Dear Balint:

I am left wondering how you felt about last night.[1] Perhaps in some ways you felt satisfied, but it is always very difficult to know what the net result is of a meeting in the Society. As I was not one of the speakers I thought I would like to write a line.

For me, your paper divides itself absolutely into two parts. It might be possible that by bringing the two parts into one paper you confuse the issue a little, and because the paper was so long it was especially difficult to discuss the total implications of it. Almost the whole of the paper seemed to me to do with the history of psycho-analytic theory. I very much envy the way you can draw on your knowledge of Freud's writings and can discuss these matters with a good deal of experience of the way things developed in fairly early days. I simply cannot take part in this kind of an exercise, although I can see its importance. Perhaps I would like to say that whereas I used to be absolutely unable to take part in a metapsychological discussion, I am now just beginning to be able to see a glimmer of light, so that if I live long enough I feel I might be able to join in from time to time. I do feel, however, that I shall always think that it is relatively unimportant the way Freud contradicted himself and gradually stimulated thought by making new suggestions. In a decade or two the people who mind about this will all be dead.

The last part of your paper shows that you are not just one of these people and that you are interested actually in babies as well as in the theory of early mechanisms. You have always made this quite clear and if you had only left out the whole of the theoretical discussion about the use of the word narcissism I think you could have continued with your claims for a recognition of what you call primary love and given us a chance to discuss it. I would personally like to discuss this very much indeed.

Although we work from completely different angles and I think we have been uninfluenced by each other, you and I are both interested in the early environmental provision. I think we agree about what happens when there is a failure. Your word basic fault comes in here and I have had my own way of talking about these things. No doubt your statement of these matters preceded mine by many years. Where I find myself disagreeing with you is on the positive side and I must say that I really don't know the answer. That is why a discussion would be so interesting, but we shall never have time for it if we must first of all decide what Freud thought about narcissism. I personally wonder very much whether an infant is aware when the environment is satisfactory, and I have actually stated in positive terms that I think that the infant is not aware of this early environmental provision but is affected when it fails. For this reason I am unable to use the word primary love here because I cannot see that there is a relationship. The infant has not yet established the capacity to make relationships and in fact is not there to be related except in an unintegrated way.

I become more definitely in disagreement with you when you use the word harmonious in description of the relationship which you call primary love. As soon as the word harmonious is used I feel I do know that a highly complex and sophisticated defence organization is at work in the child who is no longer a newly born baby or a pre-natal infant. It is this sort of thing that I would very much like to have discussed last night, because in this sort of way the theories that appeal to you and the theories that appeal to me seem to meet and then diverge.

I do hope that you did enjoy the evening although from my point of view it was in many ways a frustrating one and I still think that you have not done yourself justice in the Society for quite a long time.

Every good wish,
Yours,
D. W. Winnicott.

1. Dr. Balint had read "Primary Narcissism and Primary Love."

79 ❧ To Jacques Lacan

11th February 1960.
Dear Dr. Lacan,

I am very glad to have the fifth volume of La Psychanalyse and I write to thank you for your publication of a translation of my paper on Transitional Objects. It seems to me that someone has taken immense trouble over the details of translation and this was probably yourself. In any case I owe to you the fact that this article is now available in the French language.

I have been working at your paper on the Theory of Symbolism in memory of Ernest Jones, but I have not yet properly assimilated its meaning or assessed its significance.

Incidentally, my name ends in a double 't' (Winnicott) but that sort of thing doesn't worry me.

I have not forgotten that you asked if you could give a paper over here and no doubt you must feel that I have been very lazy about this. In fact you will know what I mean when I say that it was first necessary for the Society officially to ask a Member of the Société Psychoanalytique de Paris. Now I believe this has been arranged, that someone will come and lecture to us, and then we shall be free to invite you. I am sorry it has to be worked out this way, but I am also sorry about the split in French psychoanalysis and all the time wish that there could be a reunion. I am afraid that ill-feeling has developed to an extent that it can hardly be mended, but from my point of view the people on each side of the controversy are still quite human, ordinary men and women who are fighting for something that each believes to be good.

My wife and I remember with the very greatest pleasure the dinner you gave us in your flat when your daughter broke a bottle of wine in the kitchen! We wonder how she is getting on and we send you all our very best wishes.

Yours sincerely,

80 ❧ *To A. R. Luria*

7th July 1960

Dear Professor Luria,

My greetings to you with happy memories of Copenhagen in 1958. I have recently heard about you from a friend of mine, Miss Mary Waddington, who had the pleasure of meeting you in Moscow.

The reason why I am writing to you at the present time is that I am wondering whether the enclosed that I have recently written is of interest in your country. It has been translated into German and Italian and I think will be published in French and Turkish and possibly Portuguese. I would be very pleased indeed if this attempt to make a statement of The First Year of Life of an infant could find a place somewhere in the literature of your country. You will be able to judge when you read it. It interests me very much that babies are really the same everywhere.

With warmest greetings,
Yours sincerely,

81 ਇ To Wilfred R. Bion

17th November 1960.

Dear Bion:

As I said to you on the way out, I enjoyed the challenge of your paper last night.[1] The question I want to ask you is whether the psychotics on whom you are basing the ideas are people that you would think of as having had the capacity to dream and having lost it? Alternatively are they people who have never achieved this elbow room between the concrete and the abstract, or between psychic reality and external reality? If the former is the case, I suppose these patients have memories of dreaming and this must make a difference.

I expect that the right answer to all this will be that you are not talking directly about clinical work, but nevertheless it seems to me that you invite us to wonder whether the state of affairs which we recognise quite easily has an etiology. Another way of getting at this point would be to ask you what it is in the analysis that may possibly enable a patient who cannot dream and who cannot either sleep or wake to achieve at last the dream?

I hope you will understand that I am not expecting you to write a letter answering these questions. It is simply that I wanted to write you and put into question form the place where I was able to come into contact with your paper last night. I know that I have not been able to assimilate yet the more important aspects. Perhaps the most important thing that you are doing is to begin to deal with the challenge of the psychiatrists who could turn us all into scientific research workers and we don't know how to say why it is that we hope this won't happen. You have suggested that our attitude must eventually [address] the whole question of scientific proof.

Thank you for a very good evening.

Yours sincerely,

1. "A Theory of Functions."

82 ⦿ To Masud Khan

26th June 1961.

Dear Masud,

INTEGRATION.

Thank you for the copy of what you sent to Dr. Frankl.

At the bottom of page 1 there is something that I first felt to be misleading, but I see that you are really quoting from me. It has to do with the word dissociation which I thought should read disintegration.

I think that the word *integration* describes the developmental tendency and the achievement in the healthy individual in which he or she becomes an integer. Thus integration acquires a time-dimension. (Depressive Position, Chapter XXI.) The state prior to integration I call *unintegration*. In psycho-pathology there is *disintegration,* which is a defence, a fragmentation of the personality produced and maintained in avoidance of the destructiveness which is inherent in object-relationship after fusion (of erotic and destructive elements).

Then also there is *dissociation,* which is a rather sophisticated kind of splitting in which the total personality does not split. This is not so much "the pathological counterpart of unintegration" as a sophisticated form of disintegration. Unintegration seems to me to describe a primitive state, or else a state that is associated clinically with regression to dependence. Dissociation (like disintegration and splitting) seems to be a defence organization.

You could put: "In this paper you will find a discussion of integration and of unintegration which precedes integration, and also of disintegration which indicates a breakdown of integration. On page 151 there is a development of the theme in terms of dissociation, which is assumed to be a defence organization."

Yours,

D. W. Winnicott.

83 * To Wilfred R. Bion

16th November 1961.

My dear Bion,

I want to let you know how much I value the work you are doing and presenting to us in your papers on thinking. Like a lot of other people, I find them difficult, but extremely important. At the next meeting when your paper is discussed I may find I want to say something.

I am trying to work out the relationship between your statement and the effort I made to account for the intellectual processes as a means employed by the baby for lessening the narcissistic wound of the reality principle by understanding in localised ways the reasons for the mother's failure to adapt immediately and completely.

I know that your statement does contain something new to me and vitally important and it is this that I am trying to work out. Naturally I start from my own language in the same way that you start from yours.

Thanking you again,
Yours,

84 * To Benjamin Spock

9th April 1962.

COMMENTS ON:
Observations on the Striving for Autonomy
and some Regressive Object Relationships
after six months of age
by Benjamin SPOCK, M.D.

I am very interested in the subjects raised in your paper. No doubt you will agree that here we are touching on a vast area for our exploration. I think you will have gathered from my paper on Transitional Objects and Transitional Phenomena that I feel that we must include the infant's interest in transitional objects in our concept of normality. The use of transitional or regressive objects is so nearly universal that it would be wrong to think of abnormality when we see an infant with such an object. We could easily agree, however, that there *can* be abnormality in the non-employment of these transitional techniques and also in their employment. It is difficult to detect what is abnormal, and I think that a simple observation of an infant will not give all the clues. The clues must come from a study of the infant-mother relationship, and this must take into account the emotional state of the mother.

I am saying something very obvious to yourself but nevertheless something which must be stated from time to time, when I say that the mother can be what I call "good-enough," or even a bad mother. In the latter case the mother may be anxious or depressed and preoccupied or worried in a hypochondriacal way or depersonalised, and all these things have an effect on the infant and the way the infant finds it safe or unsafe to let the mother give ego support in the very earliest stages. (Of course if the mother is ill enough the infant at the very beginning is distorted in a way from which there can be no recovery, at any rate as far as we can see, because at the beginning the infant has not been able to organise defences). Some of my most hopeless cases have had mothers who alternate between interference and neglect. One is left with the impression that if only a mother will stay constant she can even be rather ill and yet the infant can come to gain control over this adverse environmental factor by acquaintance with it.

Your observations are very interesting and are founded on team work and organised research. I do feel like taking this opportunity to make one or two comments of a general kind. I am wondering whether you remember the analytic attitude towards infancy which I think led to a sort of stalemate somewhere in the thirties. I am thinking of the tendency among analysts to talk about infancy in terms of *satisfaction* or *frustration*. In case-history after case-history one found references to infancy in broad details of such a kind that those of us who had been engaged in paediatrics found rather cramping. I think for instance that it is very important, as you say, to consider the child's relationship to the thumb or to a transitional object in terms of *the control of the object*. In regard to thumb-sucking, I find it important to remember that the infant is holding the object at the junction of the external world and the inner world. In other words, keeping control over the object. If it goes away, it is lost (from the point of view of being controlled) whether it goes away with the mother or goes inside. (By inside I mean that it is physiologically swallowed, or eaten, or in a psychological sense incorporated or at a later stage introjected.) The transitional object, therefore, is like the thumb in that it is under control and its position is known. Nevertheless it has a richer symbolic meaning than the thumb has for the healthy infant.

When we speak of a transitional object we are thinking of an infant of at least five months and probably of a year or two old, and by this age in the infant's development there is an internal version of the mother in the healthy infant, and this can be re-exported in terms of the transitional object. In this way if the mother disappears over a long period of time, first of all the internal version of the mother dies and the child has a depressed mood, and following closely on this the transitional object and all derivatives from it lose meaning. So we have to say that if the infant is well enough, (and by this we mean that the mother is good enough as well as referring to the personal state of the infant) the fist and the thumb and the objects that are held and used enable the child to get the control over objects that are beginning to be recognised as 'not-me.' This gradually becomes a more obvious thing when it is thought of in terms of the anal stage and the control of faeces, as you have mentioned in your paper.

I would find it easier if you could incorporate into your statement something which allows for the state of the mother when she is *not* altogether satisfactory as a mother (perhaps with this particular infant or at this particular time, or in a general way so that all her children are affected). I feel that it is difficult to speak about the abnormalities in a child's use of transitional or regressive objects unless account is taken of the mother's psychology or psychiatric state. On the assumption that the mother is what I call good-enough, one can think of transitional objects and phenomena as representing the infant's beginnings in the art of the use of symbols. Where the mother is not so healthy, then one can see how the mother plays her part when either the infant avoids using these objects or alternatively uses them obsessively. I think each of these extremes is interesting and no doubt you have many observations around this sort of idea or concept. Roughly speaking, one can remember many cases in which the mother is unable to get a child to use something to stand for her; one can see that she is consciously trying to get separate from the infant, because of something in herself which does not fully understand and also because she wants to see her infant developing his or her autonomy. Being a depressive, however, she develops an unconscious protection of her child from her repressed negative affect, and one can see her placing objects in between herself and the child with the intention of effecting a separation. A bottle can be used in this way, but of course it is different according to whether the bottle has been provided from the beginning or is provided at a later date as a substitute for the breast. Infants of 10 months or so can develop a very strong need for the mother's actual body, to catch hold of her finger or her ear or her hair, and to refuse any substitute, because they know in some sort of way that if they lose their mother they lose her interest, and *she becomes preoccupied with something else;* in fact, preoccupied with her own hypochondriacal anxiety objects. They refuse to be fobbed off and to get separate the mother needs first to abandon herself to her infant's needs, and to become truly "on demand" for a while.

At the other extreme is the infant who finds relief in something that comes in between the infant and the mother. You yourself, I feel fairly sure, have written about infants who find relief in being put in the cot instead of held, and in some cases they find the impersonal cot a great relief from needing to be constantly aware of the feelings of the mother, who is anxious or is overcompensating against negative feelings or is liable to become preoccupied and to give the infant a feeling of being dropped. Infants who have come a long way with a mother and who have found it difficult to deal with her temperament may welcome the intermediate object on this account, as it is something that comes in between, whether this be a bottle or a toy or something which we can call a regressive object. Nevertheless in such cases the use of the regressive object has the makings of a pathological duality in it. Instead of being part of the infant's enriching life that comes with the establishment of the autonomy to which you are referring in this paper, in these cases the object becomes fixed; only itself can be of use, and there is lacking the general development out of the regressive object into the whole world of speech and toys and dolls and playing and reading and cultural life generally.

Perhaps you will see from what I am saying that I do find the subject a very rich one for the investigator. I wish to emphasize that I value the stress you put on the baby's determination to outgrow the symbiotic relationship when the time comes. As a patient of mine said to me recently, "You know I did have to get away from mother, quite apart from the Oedipus Complex." Naturally, as you would expect, in this analysis there was *also* the Oedipus complex to be negotiated, but the fact remained and has been established in this analysis (if one needs to quote one case) that the baby who is healthy is determined to outgrow what sometimes is called the symbiotic relationship. But I am not really very fond of this term, symbiotic relationship. I feel that there is a very great difference between the infant's dependence on the mother (dependence here meaning that the ego of the infant is strong only because of the mother's ego support, the mother being good-enough) and the mother's part in what is called the symbiotic relationship. The mother's part is a very much more sophisticated affair and depends on her being able to become preoccupied towards the end of her pregnancy and at the beginning of the life of the infant with her infant, so that she is able to identify with the infant in a highly sensitive way, using her experiences and her imagination. Because of this capacity of the mother (who is good-enough at mothering) to identify in this way she is able to start the infant off with the capacity to be "determined to outgrow the symbiotic relationship." But first there must have been this special state of affairs which belongs to the earliest possible stage. Another reason why I am *not* fond of the term symbiotic relationship is that the term gives no indication of why the relationship should ever end, except that the *infant* wants it to end. Actually in my opinion the mother's special state in which she is able to identify closely with her infant only belongs to the few months just before the birth and after the birth, and the *mother* tends to recover from this state and to need the infant to become autonomous. This is the other half of that which you are referring to by the words "the baby's determination to outgrow" etc. etc.

You will see how keen I am to allow for the mother's state at this early stage in which the infant really is entirely dependent on the mother for starting off with the capacity which turns into his determination to outgrow etc. etc. I know that in saying this I am not saying anything which runs counter to the work which you have published and which has had so great a value all over the world. As for me, I have tried to put this point of view of mine in many papers but particularly I have tried to give it in my broadcast talks called The Ordinary Devoted Mother which now appear in the book "The Child and the Family."

I must ask you to forgive me if in making these notes I have seemed to talk rather dogmatically. I know what a tremendous amount of thought you have given to all these matters relating to the infant-mother partnership. I too am very interested in all the details and it would be very important from my point of view if one day we could have time for a fairly organised discussion. Actually I shall be in U.S.A. in October and in Cambridge for about ten days (17th–26th). It will not be possible for me, as far as I can see, to fit in a visit to Cleveland, as your distances are tremendous in your country and there will be plenty for me to do if I am to see my friends. I shall be staying with Dr. Elizabeth Zetzel. One day I do hope, however, to try to make a contact with yourself, that is to say if you are willing.

D. W. Winnicott.

P.S. I am sending you my book The Child and the Family which I like better than its U.S.A. version "Mother and Child" (Basic Books Inc.) and I have instructed Basic Books to send you a copy of my Collected Papers.

85 ❧ *To Ronald McKeith*

31st January 1963.

Dear Ronald:

It was good of you to send me a copy of your book, which I am glad to have. I shall read it and I expect I shall enjoy it.

In order to maintain the friendly feeling that I have towards you,

I am writing this letter critically. I want to say that it is not good your writing me a letter to say that I have had some influence on the relationship between paediatrics and child psychiatry in this country when in fact you scotomize me and my writings in the book. Your reference to my very immature early paper of 1934 would certainly not give a reader coming to this field the idea that I had started to have an influence on things somewhere later than that date and that I have written quite a lot which could easily have been referred to in your book. There are chapters in my Collected Papers which are quite relevant to your subject, and you could very easily have put this in to give readers the recommendation. I think I would mind being left out very much if I were to suppress this letter. Having written it, however, I feel the matter is closed and I am now free to enjoy the book as a positive contribution to the subject.

Every good wish, and success to the book,

Yours,

86 ᴇ≫ To Timothy Raison

9th April 1963.
Dear Mr. Raison,

Questionnaire.

This letter is not the sort of answer you wanted. I am simply writing to say that I have not filled in the survey because I am allergic to all this type of investigation. Obviously this means an emotional reaction on my part but perhaps I could say one of the reasons why I do not like these forms. I think the best people find it very difficult to answer this sort of survey and this is because they feel at a fairly deep level and they cannot go over the ground covered by this survey without taking a very long time considering each item. They have to be able to reach an answer creatively. What in fact happens is that they do not bother to do this (as indeed they could not do because of the time factor). They therefore answer superficially and using the top layer of their intellectual apparatus, and this has practically no value. Moreover this kind of reaction gives the wrong answers and the electronic apparatus which very cleverly sorts out the answers given works to no avail because it is working with a vast collection of flimsy elements. The whole thing is like building a house on sand, to use a rather old-fashioned simile. The results of course look impressive.

For me the whole thing is thoroughly bad except when it is a Christmas-time game to be enjoyed and forgotten.

You wanted to know my view and I am giving it to you.

> With good wishes,
> Yours sincerely,
> D. W. Winnicott, F.R.C.P.

87 ᵽ *To the Editor,* New Society

23rd March 1964.

Dear Sir,

Love or Skill

It interests me that your journal has found a wide public for the consideration of problems that are somewhat specialised, such as that raised by Paul Halmos (March 19th). What indeed is the prime factor in social work of all kinds, including psychoanalysis? As my name was mentioned several times I wish to take up the theme where Mr. Halmos leaves it.

Social work is professional work, and what is being discussed is the motivation that applies in the limited area of the worker's relation to a client-situation. It can certainly be held that love is necessary; the work could not be done out of hate. But the worker's hate is contained in the structure of the professional relationship, its finite nature, its being paid for, etc. If the word love is used the most primitive meanings of the word must be included, in which love is crude and ruthless and even destructive. Hate is not absent but it is sublimated. This is important because, in my view, there is great danger in a dissemination of a sentimental idea about psycho-analysis, social work, or being a parent.

Mr. Halmos did not develop the concept of diagnosis in his

short article. However, these matters cannot be discussed without reference to diagnosis. Character disorder, or the antisocial grouping, is related to environmental failure of a relatively obvious kind, and very subtle environmental factors are important in the etiology of disorders of personality. I have found it to be important to point this out to psycho-analysts, who till recently have concerned themselves chiefly with internal strains and stresses. In so far as I am trying to inform social investigators and the public generally, however, I try to draw attention to the internal and personal factors in individuals whose illnesses are psychological, because the tendency is always to get away from personal pain and internal conflict to social persecution and to failure of the family function. I shudder lest my work should be taken as a weighting on the environmental side on the scales of argument, although I do hold the view that psycho-analysis can afford now to give full importance to external factors, both good and bad, and especially to the part played by the mother at the very beginning when the infant has not yet separated out the not-me from the me.

In fact, love does not "cure" in the social work or psycho-analytic senses. Therapy of this simple kind only applies if we are foster parents or house mothers, and we have not chosen to do this kind of work, nor are we (probably) fitted to do it. In social work (as in psycho-analysis) certain factors such as reliability, dependability, objectivity, provide a specialised environment *over a period of time* in which the highly complex *internal* factors in the individual and between the various individuals in the client group may rearrange themselves. The "good" (or I would say "good enough") climate enables a client to review his or her relationship to climates that were not, or did not seem to be, good (or good enough). Moreover, in complex cases where deprivation has been a factor, there develop bad periods in the social-work situation in which the client remembers by reliving awful periods that have been experienced in the past. Social workers have to be able to endure these bad times and wait for a recovery, which does in fact often come.

In a psycho-analytic treatment there is added a variable quantity of interpretation of that in the individual which is just ready to become conscious, or to be remembered; but in the type of case that is suitable for social work these interpretations are unnecessary. From social work the psycho-analyst can learn (among other things) that interpretation is not the most important part of the work in those cases in which environmental failure is relatively important in the etiology. In the treatment of psychoneurosis, the proper field for classical psycho-analysis, the important etiological factors are those of internal conflict, not of environmental failure, and in such work interpretation of that which, day by day, is just ready for becoming conscious, remains the staple diet, so to speak. And no one would object, surely, if by increased knowledge the psycho-analyst should know better and better what verbal interpretation he might have made at the times when he deemed it unnecessary or even unwise to speak.

I hope that Mr. Halmos will not consider that I have contradicted his main thesis; rather I have tried to develop his theme in a manner that may lead to fruitful discussion, but away from the danger of sentimentality. Also, social work is not religion.

Yours etc.
D. W. Winnicott, F.R.C.P.

88 ❧ *To the* Observer

12th October 1964.

As I have been quoted in the original article by Martin James, "The Mothers Children Need," I would like to take part in this discussion of what children need of their mothers. Of all that could be said, I wish to attempt to separate out certain concepts which tend to get mixed up with each other in a discussion. I have expressed the view that what a baby needs of the mother at the very beginning, that is to say, just before birth and just after, is something which has very little, if anything at all, to do with cleverness. It seems to me fairly obvious that what the baby needs is more of the nature of the capacity on the part of the mother to give full attention. I have brought in the word *devotion* here at risk, because there are some who associate this word with sentimentality. It is probable that there is very full agreement as far as this goes, and in my own researches I find that it is a failure in this respect that predisposes to autism, sometimes called infantile schizophrenia. The opposite of devotion is lack of devotion or an inability on the part of the mother to give herself over for a few weeks to this special function of hers. A mother who keeps a certain proportion of herself uninvolved throughout the later stages of pregnancy and the early stages immediately following the birth of the infant does, according to my researches, run the risk of interfering with the infant's processes of emotional growth in such a way that there is a liability to illness of this variety that is labelled autism. She may, of course, get around this difficulty by employing someone to act for her at this stage, and giving the baby over to the care of a nurse who can perform this function for her, and the result can be satisfactory.

Confusion, I suggest, arises from the idea that the opposite of devotion is cleverness. I would take it for granted that it is a good thing if an infant's mother has an I.Q. that is at least average, and certainly the advantage must show at a later date in the child's development. It would seem to me to be quite compatible with a high I.Q. if a mother is able to do this thing which I am calling giving herself over to a function for a limited period of a few weeks when this is what is needed of her.

It is of course possible that a woman endowed with a high intellectual capacity may have developed a way of existing which exploits her capacity and which involves the use of intellectual rather than of body functions. It may be more difficult for such a woman to spend a few weeks in which her special capacity is wasted.

The chief difficulty for a newborn baby arises from something quite different from the mother's intellectual capacity. It comes from her having an orientation towards some kind of career which is so important to her that she cannot let go of it. This might happen in the case of a woman with an I.Q. less than average. No disparagement of the career woman is implied if it be stated that, apparently, infants cannot make use of anything but the whole of a woman at the very beginning; if a woman cannot relinquish her hold on her career for the few vital weeks before and after parturition, then there must be expected an effect on the baby, and this effect takes the form of a failure of the maturational process at the first stage when the infant has not yet felt the mother or any part of her to be separate from himself or herself.

It will be seen that this argument, if it be valid, does not concern itself with the intellectual capacity of the woman. That the vast majority of women with careers do interrupt their careers for the short time required, just as they do let each new infant have a first experience of an only child, even when there are in fact other children.

89 ❧ To John O. Wisdom

26th October 1964.

Dear J.O.W.,

Thank you for your papers, the result of much work. I wanted to speak at the Bion meeting but a very exacting patient (really very ill) made me unable to do all the necessary homework. That's the worst of these evenings with its being taken for granted that we all know beforehand what the speaker is up to.

At present I am convalescent from two days' 'flu, which gives me some freedom to write to people and to read.

About Bion and all that. I like the way he goes ahead in his own grooves, and I'm one of those who hope for a lot from him. In writing a paper about him you have helped me to make a new effort to grip the Bion line, and for this I am grateful.

When *you write about* Bion I do not easily allow your failure to relate Bion's work to that of his colleagues, though I consider he himself has full right to go ahead without even knowing what others of us are writing, let alone putting in references.

You relate Bion's work to Freud and Klein which is the important thing. But *in your role of commentator* you do need to relate his work to contemporaries, including me. (As a matter of fact I never feel you have read anything of mine, but no matter, except to me.)

What Marion [Milner] said was just a little bit of what she felt. She is the one who has reverie in her presentation of her ideas in our Society, and remember, although she is modest she is one of the ones we have who has brains.

It is important to me that Bion states (obscurely of course) what I have been trying to state for 2½ decades but against the terrific opposition of Melanie. Bion uses the word reverie to cover the idea that I have stated in the complex way that it deserves that the infant is ready to create something, and in good-enough mother- ing *the mother lets the baby know what is being created*—of Sechehaye's term symbolic realization, i.e. in therapy. Bion says (half-way down page 36): "What happens will depend. . . . ." Melanie Klein absolutely would not allow this, and my relation to her was (though always warm and good) impaired by her adamant objec- tion to "what happens depends . . ."

You should have mentioned this fact, that Bion goes deeper than Melanie here, or finds a way of stating what Melanie would not allow.

Bion, however, finds himself in a muddle and postulates the infant's need for a breast—a "bad breast" which has to be ex- changed for a good one.

I think my way of using mother's good-enough adaptation to ego needs has something more straightforward than this, without violation of the facts and findings in direct observations and in the work of those of us who treat the occasional "borderline" case.

I like Bion's treatment of this subject, and I can learn something from it. But if you (not he) are talking about it you ought to say: this is what D.W.W. has been trying to get us to see for two or three decades. In a way, all that Bion has done is to divert our attention from the main issue to alpha and beta functions. Well, if that's his way, "that's my fancy now," as the popular song says. But you can't get away with it in your role of commentator.

Again, 84 top, Bion talks about the needed objects that tantal- ise. Now any one can use the English word tantalise, but it is I who have used it in this context. I have spoken of the worst kind of mothering, in which the mother, at the very early stage, must tantalise—that is, be unpredictable, so that she cannot even be relied on to fail to adapt to a need. From this, I have said, it is to be doubted whether a baby can recover, and in treatment this is, in my experience, the most difficult type of case.

But, for babies ordinarily held well, there is no experience of a tantalising nature. That will be met later on, but only after the basis of belief is laid down, that is, of "belief in. . . ."

As you are turning out a series of psychoanalytic statements written in the quietude (!) of family life (joke) and not written in the hurly-burly of case-involvement, we must ask of you that you be better read than we are.

I don't mind being shown to be wrong, or criticised or banged about. But I have done some important work out of the sweat of my psycho-analytic brow (i.e. clinically) and I refused to be scotomised. I hated the boxing part of the Olympic T.V. which I otherwise watched with joy, but in the Society I'm quite happy to do some boxing if you can enjoy it too.

It was awful not to get up in the Wisdom-Bion Night, but I had definitely not done enough reading whether of your paper or of Bion. I still have a lot to do on Bion, and thank you for providing the stimulus.

All the best,
Yours,

P.S. I'm reading your MS as broadcast, at this moment.

90 ❧ *To the Editor, the* Observer

5th November 1964.

Sir,

All of Mother

My letter (shortened with my agreement) carried an unfortunate implication, picked up by Mr. Baron and by A Father. I feel so far from *blaming* any parent for anything that I failed to see that someone might be hurt by what I wrote. I did not mean that autistic children have necessarily been neglected.

Autism has, of course, a complex etiology; this cannot be properly described or discussed here in this correspondence, but it needs and gets full treatment in professional debate.

It would be a pity, however, if for fear lest someone be hurt, no way could be found to express the point of view that I and some others find to be true, that an infant is fortunate if, at the very beginning, he or she can have "all of mother."

D. W. Winnicott, F.R.C.P.

91 ᕀᕀ To Mrs. B. J. Knopf

26th November 1964.

Dear Mrs. Knopf,

Your letter has been passed on to me,[1] and I am distressed that I should have muddled you up. It is silly of us to discuss medical matters that involve the use of technical terms in a paper like The Observer.

Perhaps you can forget all that about autism. What interests you is the upbringing of normal children, and I have written quite a lot about this. I enclose a book which you may or may not find interesting.

Perhaps you will do best to give up trying to work at all this, and just go on naturally enjoying your experiences. Later you may like to go back over what you experience with a book or two to guide you, but while you are having a child I think you may do best to follow your natural feelings.

If you want direct instruction you may find help from Benjamin Spock's *Baby and Child Care* (Bodley Head, London, 1955).

Let me know how you get on, and forget about that rare condition called autism.

Yours sincerely,
D. W. Winnicott, F.R.C.P.

1. A response to Winnicott's letter of 12 October 1964 in the *Observer.*

92 ᕀᕀ To Humberto Nagera

15th February 1965.

Dear Dr. Nagera:

You sent me your "Early Childhood" paper on November last. You know, it was too long for me to read, with all the things I am trying to write. I kept it on my desk, always hoping the get the necessary couple of hours, but I never reached this state.

What I have seen of the paper seems to me to be excellent. Certainly you have worked very hard at it, and I hope it brings rewards.

I hope the fact that you do not accept Melanie Klein's view of infantile neurosis will not prevent you from trying to gain something from her immense contribution to our work. You see, I feel that your reference to Klein could be based on a reading of *one page,* namely page viii of the preface to Segal's book.

I rather agree with your reference to Klein and the Infantile Neurosis, but as I worked with Melanie for some years, especially in the thirties, and learned a very great deal about children from her, I want to make sure that you are not contented with reading one page of a book about her. It is difficult to get the Klein contribution even from a study of all she herself wrote.

This is a minor matter from your point of view. The work represented here is solid and instructive and constructive. I do congratulate you.

If you had wanted to quote from me you could have done so (Chapter 1, Collected Papers; Chapter 4, Part 1, and Chapter 4, part 11, The Child and the Family) but I know this was not a place for references.

For me, however, there is a history to the position from which you are now working, and quite a few of us have contributed to the fact that you have this place in the world (London and the Psycho-Analytical Society) from which to write a paper. I hope you accept this broad comment from an older man.

I have found value in your reminding us of the continuing importance of the concept of The Infantile Neurosis in Psycho-Analytic Theory.

Forgive me for this long delay.

Yours sincerely,
D. W. Winnicott, F.R.C.P.

93 ❧ *To Michael Fordham*

24th June 1965.

Dear Michael:

I hope you were satisfied with the meeting last night. I had quite a lot of other things I would like to have said but it seemed to be important to sit down and give the meeting a chance to react to your paper in its own way. I still think we need to go on trying to make a statement of what we are aiming at doing when we treat a psychotic child. In a way your theme continued mine of a few months ago in the same room when I talked about psychotherapy in terms of two people bumping up against each other. I think we are all on to the same problems and that is what makes it so interesting.

I wanted to say something more about repetition. My case illustration was rather out of step because the patient was a different kind of case, but the pencil rolling business illustrated an aspect of repetitiveness. I think you were talking about other meanings of this word. I felt that what happened in the pencil case has to be understood in terms of the dynamics of that place into which the withdrawn child mentally withdraws. In this place dynamics is to be looked at in terms of pendulum movement. Even in stillness there is a potential pendulum movement, so that stillness alternates, as it were, from being relative to right or left. If there is no pendulum movement then there is death.

I think that this patient in the course of her recovery was able to make a relationship with me on the basis that I accepted one half of the pendulum movement, so that she could accept the other and the game had to do with establishing a relationship to the world on this basis. The normal equivalent of this from my point of view is the rocking of infant-care, and in psycho-pathology there are all the clinical rhythms of autistic children and the rocking of deprived children to be remembered.

I thought that Wisdom was on to a good thing when he drew attention to the universality of this phenomenon although perhaps he need not have gone as far away as the beaches of Alexandria; I think he could have looked into the backyards of London and no doubt he would agree. In Wimbledon week perhaps it is a good idea to remind ourselves that the important thing is just this to and fro which becomes so sophisticated in tennis but which has to do with something fundamental in object-relating. I am going to send a copy of this letter to J. O. Wisdom in case he enjoys following up this idea.

You were of course right in emphasizing the fact that sooner or later the child destroys you. I think that by the time the child gets here a great deal of work has been done and the beginning of recovery is already to be seen. This does not mean, however, to you or me, that recovery will take place, because if these very early disturbances do not occur at the very early stage where they belong, they are very difficult indeed to accommodate clinically. Fantasy is not yet accepted and there is no hate, only murder. I feel sure that Melanie Klein was trying to deal with this in her "Envy" book, but unfortunately for those of us who like exploring, she failed in some important respect when she jumped the gun and went back over the realities of dependence to heredity.

What I have written reminds me of what I remember of the Autocrat at the Breakfast Table.

> Every good wish,
> Yours,
> D. W. Winnicott.

94 ❧ To Michael Fordham

15th July 1965.

Dear Michael:

Thank you for your further letter about autism. It is not an easy letter to assimilate or even to understand, because you typed it just as you were thinking it, but I shall keep it. I am sure that it really does contain the sort of ideas which germinate.

Yes, there is a tremendous difference between rolling a pencil to and fro between a patient and oneself and the endless rocking or rolling of pencils or whatever happens that goes on without relationships. As you say, the child is beginning to get better when there is a communication through one of these primitive repetitions. I know an autistic child who was treated by very clever interpretations and who has done moderately well. What started off the treatment, however, was something which the first analyst did, and it is strange that I have never been able to get the second analyst to acknowledge the importance of what I will describe. The first analyst, Dr. Maida Hall, died. Dr. Hall found this boy who had gone autistic after being normal and sat in the room with him and established a communication by doing everything that this boy did. He would sit for ¼ hour still, and then move his foot a little; she would move her foot. His finger would move and she would imitate, and this went on for a long time. Out of these beginnings everything showed signs of developing until she died. If I could have got the clever analyst to join on to all this I think we might by now have had something like a cure instead of having to put up with one of those maddening cases where a lot of good work has been done and everybody is very pleased but the child is not satisfactory.

I hope you and Frieda have a good holiday.

All for now,
Yours,

95 ᵉᵛ *To Charles Anthony Storr*

30th September 1965.
Dear Dr. Storr:

I was glad to meet you and also I was interested in what you were saying. Isn't the clue (in part) that in the west, which is a depressive society, paranoids hide their delusions, or else hide them in systems, and if they can't, well then they are "mad." By contrast, in Nigeria Society, "based on projection," the delusions arising out of projection simply narrow down the circle of the man (or woman)'s friends to those who have similar delusions. No doubt the very deluded get fairly near to being isolated. But never quite, perhaps.

Isn't it awful to think that the west has introduced barbaric ECT to a community that was getting on quite well with healers, who are psychologically minded in a sophisticated way, even if rather magical and unscientific.

Good wishes,
Yours,

96 ໕ To the Editor, the Times

3rd March 1966.

Sir,

Psychiatric Care

Some important observations on the matter raised in Professor Hill's letter (23rd February) have been made (Dr. Guy Mitchell, Mr. Robert Humphreys). Among other issues relative to the lack of mental hospital provision for the adolescent are the following:

I have been involved and have watched this problem over several decades and there is no reason why there should ever be any outcome. Partly the difficulty arises out of the peculiar nature of mental disorder in the adolescent period, this being difficult to distinguish clinically from the difficulties inherent in the adolescent phase of growth towards independence, and partly the difficulties arise out of there being no professional body that feels responsible. In other words, child psychiatry must urgently become a discipline with its own autonomy since experience has proved that neither paediatrics nor psychiatry (of adults) has the will or the specific knowledge necessary for professional involvement in this vast area of care. In fact, the treatment (and prevention) of emotional disorder in childhood has been done and will be done by psychiatric social workers, child care officers (Children's Committee), and Probation Officers, and the whole community of residential workers in boarding schools for difficult (ill) children. It is now too late for either psychiatry or paediatrics to claim an interest in our specialty. We must go ahead with only a friendly liaison with the two established disciplines, and plan according to the needs which only we know.

In a detail, we need and have needed now for thirty years an experimental hostel or boarding school for half a dozen children to be located in the area in which psycho-analysts live and work. Only in this way can a beginning be made to the problem of the treatment of those children of any age who need treatment of two kinds at once, treatment by specialised management and treatment by intensive personal therapy.

To what Ministry can one turn for support for even this limited and preliminary work which would set a pattern, in the course of a decade, for expansion of provision and for the training of personnel?

Yours faithfully,
D. W. Winnicott, F.R.C.P.

97 ᶜ To Herbert Rosenfeld

17th March 1966.
Dear Dr. Rosenfeld:

I am grateful to you for reacting to my remark last night at Thorner's paper. There must be many who got something valuable out of what you said.

(By way of further comment, I think the subject is not exhausted even by your statement. Incidentally I remember Clare telling me that in a supervision you said to her "the analyst must not be afraid to take the patient's projections.") What I have in mind is that there are some cases in which the analyst is able to accept these projections without in any way endangering the total transference framework. I am referring to certain patients who, in the localised area of a short phase of analysis are very ill indeed and they cannot stand the gap between the blunt experience and the psycho-analytic interpretation. In other words for such patients at such times the analyst, in conveying through interpretations that he accepts the patient's projections, is in fact being reasonable, but not deeply enough understanding. I have a patient like this at the present time, an adolescent girl, and the phases only last about twenty minutes. In those minutes I become a worse persecutor the more reasonable I show myself to be. The patient recovers mercifully before going home.

From this it follows that I am not happy about Thorner's title Cause and Reason, and I think you were not happy either. I suppose he is talking about aetiology as compared with all the other things like the sense of responsibility.

I think what I am saying is this. I would like to hear it discussed how when a patient's mother was mad, does the patient bring this into the transference? It is not true that at some moment or other the patient must find that the analyst is mad? These considerations do not of course affect the ordinary case on which we teach psycho-analysis.

I am not expecting you to answer this kind of rambling letter but I just felt like writing it . . .

Yours sincerely,
D. W. Winnicott.

98 ᏋᏅ *To Hans Thorner*

17th March 1966.

Dear Hans,

I hope you were pleased with the reception of your paper last night.[1] It was very interesting and important.

In regard to the tiny detail that I threw in at the end, this certainly did not call for a reply. I would like to say, however, that it is very confusing in the Society when various terms are used as if they were fully accepted. I am sure you know exactly what you mean when you say: "dangerous parts. . . . . derivatives of the death instinct. . . . . must be expelled" etc. etc. I myself do not know what you mean and at least half the Society will feel that you are simply saying "death instinct" instead of using the words "aggression" and "hate." You may feel this is very unimportant, as indeed it is in the context of your paper, but it would be really valuable in the Society if we could find a common language. Sometime or other when you have nothing to do would you feel like rewriting that sentence without using the words "death instinct," just for my benefit?

Thanking you again for the paper,

Yours,

1. "Cause or Reason: A Psychoanalytical Contribution to the Understanding of Psychosomatic Phenomena."

99 ⮾ *To a Confidant*

15th April 1966.

Dear M:

Thank you for your postcard. I think that you know the answer to your question because you have been in a state of primary maternal preoccupation relative to your new baby, and from what you write you seem to have enjoyed the experience. Anthropologically you would recognise this under the term couvade, but it seems rather nasty to give a name to something that is being experienced in the present.

I wonder whether you can make use of this idea. Everybody is bisexual in the sense of the capacity to identify with man and woman. There is a great difference, however, between a unified personality such as that of a man with a capacity for identification with a woman, and a similar but different thing, a male man with a split off woman self. I have tried to refer to this in a paper which is not published but which you could look at if you liked, in which I talk about the male and female elements in men and women. Others of course have written on the same subject.

What strikes me is that in your own development you may be in the process of changing over from being a male with a split off woman self to being a more integrated individual containing all the elements including the two identifications.

I think that the study of man's identification with woman has been very much complicated by a persistent attempt on the part of psycho-analysts to call everything that is not male in a man homosexuality, whereas in fact homosexuality is a secondary matter or less fundamental and rather a nuisance when one is trying to get at man's woman identification.

I don't know whether you can make anything of this very condensed note but in any case there is always the waste paper basket!

Good wishes,
Yours sincerely,
D. W. Winnicott, F.R.C.P.

100 ❧ *To Lili E. Peller*

15th April 1966.

Dear Miss Peller:

In this letter I am trying to reply to the first paragraph of your letter of 28th March. It may seem rather strange that I should make this big distinction between desire and need. Nevertheless in my contact with the psycho-analytic society I was constantly in a state of frustration up till about 1944 because in the Scientific Meetings of the Society I constantly heard references to wishes, and I found that this was being used as a defence blocking the study of need. As a paediatrician I came to psycho-analysis very much aware of infantile dependence, and I found it exasperating that the only dependence my colleagues could envisage was dependence on the kind of provision that leads to id satisfactions. I took part in altering this, at least in so far as the British Society is concerned. On many occasions I drew attention to the fact that speakers were referring to infancy as if the beginning was a matter of instinct gratification. Gradually I found Miss Freud, and then others, using the word need, but it is a slow business and this same thing is at the root of one of our present troubles in the whole psycho-analytic movement.

Progress in the study of what a psycho-analyst can do in reference to borderline and schizoid personalities depends more than anything else on the recognition of dependence as something that refers to need. For instance, in anorexia nervosa and the common anorexias that have the same psychopathology, oral satisfaction has become a dissociated phenomenon, a kind of seduction. What is more important to the child is *not eating,* which at any rate leaves the child unseduced and existing as an individual (even if dying).

In my more recent writings you have noticed that I have tried to enumerate the psychotic-type anxieties which cluster round the word need. These have nothing to do with instincts. They have to do with such things as disintegration, depersonalization, the opposite of progress in emotional development, that is to say, annihilation, falling for ever, lack of contact with not-me objects, etc. You will find reference to this, for instance, in my book in the Hogarth Press (The Maturational Processes and the Facilitating Environment).

It would interest me to have your reaction to this reply that I am trying to make to your letter. It may be that you have already discussed these matters in the papers you have sent me which I must study. The trouble is that there is so much of importance which one has no time to read. I am very interested indeed in this problem which you refer to in your letter.

> With every good wish,
> Yours sincerely,
> D. W. Winnicott, F.R.C.P.

101 ❧ *To Sylvia Payne*

26th May 1966.

Dear Sylvia:

Thank you for your letter.[1] I will go into the whole matter again. You do realize, don't you, that the Scientific Bulletin has a limited circulation and is not a publication? Also there is quite a big change in the atmosphere in the Society at the present time, especially among the bulk, that is to say those who came into the Society after all these troubles had become history.

I am sorry that you have been shocked and startled. Sometimes it is difficult to steer an even course between doing nothing and doing something. I will write again.

> Yours,

1 Dr. Payne had strenuously objected to the printing of the Controversial Discussions of 1943 that led to the subdivision of training groups in the British Institute.

102 ❧ *To Donald Meltzer*

25th October 1966.

Dear Donald,

Thank you for your paper[1] and the contribution it made to the scientific work of the Society. As I said before, I am glad you wrote on this subject. It was satisfactory from my point of view that most of the speakers except Money-Kyrle were not Kleinians. From the chair one gets an over-all view of the functioning of the Society and it happens that if I look back on the last six scientific meetings the Kleinian contingent was either absent or else disappeared before the discussion in all the papers except that of Betty Joseph. As you remember, on that occasion the whole Kleinian contingent gathered together to give her support which she did not in fact need any more than you did.

I said I would like to write you about a few details and if I write now it will be simply a matter of bits and pieces. If I wait, however, I may find that there is too long an interval. Most of what I say will probably be critical because I am not writing to discuss what I feel to be good about your paper.

I really do feel worried about your reference in the middle of page 4 to dependence on the *internal* mother. I would like to suggest that this is sloppy thinking. The foundation of stable and healthy psychic structure is certainly related to a dependability of the internal mother, but this dependability is itself maintained by the individual. It is true that people spend their lives holding up the lamp-post that they are leaning against, but somewhere at the beginning there has to be a lamp-post on its own, otherwise, there is no introjection of dependability.

As I am writing this I can see that you may claim that the words *dependence of the infantile parts of the self on the internal mother* may be felt by you to cover this point, but I raise the matter because you bring in the word internal mother again near the top of page 6 and I felt that here you could have left out the word internal.

It seems to me that by exploiting to the full the useful concept of the internal object you lose the infinite richness which is subsumed in the word fantasy. Fantasy not only allows for all degrees from conscious to unconscious but it also has room for the concept of an infinite series of fantasies co-existent and possibly dissimilar or opposite.

You must not feel that I am attacking the idea of the individual having a delusion that ideas have an existence in their head or belly, and I believe that there is a lot to be got out of this kind of way of thinking, exactly as a child gets value from playing with toys. But the game that your child is playing this morning, although very rich, is poor as compared with the total fantasy of which it is a local representative. I cannot see what is to be lost by saying that a house, in the case of your patient and in the case of most people, is a symbol of the mother.

Incidentally, I am longing for the day when one of the Kleinian group will be able to say that the dependability of the internal mother has a history in the actual dependability at the beginning, but Melanie Klein would not allow this. She would only say: "Of course I have always said that environment is important"—and imply thereby that she would be giving away something vital if she were to say what I have just put down in words. Bion seems to me to be the only Kleinian who has used a sentence which amounts to the same thing as what I have just written. Actually I know that you did not have to commit yourself in this respect in this paper because you were not dealing with this particular subject. If, however, the dependability of the internal figures does not derive from actual experience in early infantile life then one can say also that it does not matter whether the analyst is dependable or lacks dependability, and I feel that we cannot hold this view.

To return to your paper: you do know, I suppose, that on page 3 when you use the word envy you are suddenly talking to a limited audience, namely the Kleinian group, and that the rest of the room is out of touch with you. This seems to me to be a great pity because one cannot always draw attention to these things which members of the Kleinian group tend to do as if they were determined to carry the point by propaganda, that is to say by repetition. You will agree, I think, that it is not possible for a Kleinian to use the word envy in the ordinary way that everyone uses the word unless this is specifically stated. If a Kleinian uses the word envy then this word carries the implication of acceptance of Melanie's Geneva paper (later her book), namely that the roots of aggression are linked with envy which accounts for the infant's impulse to destroy the good breast. It is the Kleinian group who feel that this makes sense and the whole of the rest of your audience feels irritated because for them the introduction of the word envy at this point in the search for the origins of aggression does not add anything at all but confuses the issue by ascribing to the newborn infant this very complex thing that we mean by envy. So suddenly on page 3 you push three-quarters of your audience away, hoping they will come back to listen to the rest of your paper.

The same would be true if you were to use the words death instinct, taking for granted that this invention of Freud's has value. If you ignore these very big divisions of opinion you are setting up barriers between yourself and the audience, and free discussion gradually becomes impossible. It would be perfectly all right, of course, if the paper were about envy (or about the death instinct) but you were writing about adult sexuality and these things were thrown in in this way that irritates us beyond description. You know what I mean: a whole list of them including projective identification.

One wonders indeed what sort of analyses Melanie Klein must have been doing in all those years before she made pronouncements about these essential points of belief. Actually as one who was in touch with her before the war I can say that she did very good and interesting work before these ideas turned up. She was always having ideas, of course, and they were tremendously important to her when she had them. At one time she endeared herself to me by the concept of internal chaos because of the fact that she insisted on pronouncing this CHOUS, rhyming with the word COWS except tht the s was short and sharp! I was very close to her in those days and learned a tremendous amount from her and I refrained from correcting this one word because of her mispronunciation of it because it was such fun! By the way, in those days she used to tell me what she thought the Society needed, because she was interested in it, and she was trying to build it up as a unit. She said to me: "I hope you will always go to every meeting and stay till the end. You will not do the Society good by only going to the papers that you like." She herself followed this precept and went to every meeting except when she was unable to get out of bed if she had 'flu. I only wish that she could have said this to the present Kleinian group which is in the process of budding itself off from the Society. I do wish you could see what it looks like from the President's chair.

I seem to be in a discursive mood!—putting a strain on some aspect of your tolerance. By the way, I do not easily agree with your remark on work and play in the middle of page 5. I hope one day you will give more thought to this. It seems to me that play and work are very similar except that work is more appropriately applied as the individual becomes mature. I think by work you mean compliance and you assume some authoritative person giving directives. This, however, could also happen in play. There is something wrong there which you may be able to correct in a paper or as a chapter of a book.

While I am on page 5 could I say that I would have liked you to have developed the theme of the change that occurred in your patient and why this change did occur. You say: "The realization that . . . ." Does realization clear up something like a symptom in this way? I think that you would want to restate this in terms of the transference and the support to the ego organization which the analyst gives by his understanding and which enables the patient not only to realize something but to accept all its implications. Probably you would agree with the sort of thing I am saying here.

I was glad towards the end when you began to develop the theme of what testicles mean and the total fantasy system of human beings. There is a great deal there that I am not clear about and any contribution is of value.

. . .

Well, that is all I want to say at the moment. I suppose Balint walked out on you, if it was not just that he was tired after the interval, because you made no reference to him, and he of all analysts has really taken the trouble to write about adult sexuality. We all tend to ignore his work and personally I think that you could have mugged up something of his so as to refer to the fact that this very senior man right in front of you had been giving thought to these matters in a constructive way continuously over the past forty years.

Every good wish,
Yours,
D. W. Winnicott.

1. "The Introjective Basis of Polymorphous Tendencies in Adult Sexuality."

103 ᚦ To a Patient

13th December 1966.

Dear Mrs. N:

Thank you for your letter. I do find it very difficult to advise you. Even to see you once would be very difficult for me at the present time. I wonder if you would like to get an interview with one of my colleagues . . .

From your description it seems as if you are beginning to feel real especially in relation to your painting, and it seems to me to be of little importance in these experiences whether you are in the present or in your childhood or in your infancy. It is just here that the various dates join up together like the parts of an old-fashioned telescope. There is always the possibility of course that it is best not to see anyone at all but to carry on, hoping that someone will look at your paintings and judge them not in the way you do as a kind of therapeutics, but as paintings. In this way you may find some of them on a wall somewhere with people looking at them, but course these will be the ones in which you have managed to disguise the bit that is important to you.

Let me know what happens.

Yours sincerely,
D. W. Winnicott, F.R.C.P.

104 ᚦ To D. N. Parfitt

22nd December 1966.

Dear Dr. Parfitt,

I was glad to see your letter in the B.M.J. 24th December. There seems to be no limit to the territory bagged by Dr. Sargant and those who seem to have a need to deny the existence of dynamic psychology.[1] I shall probably not write myself simply because one gets tired of taking up these points one by one.

It is of course true that anorexia cases can be very serious and that in the course of giving psychotherapy or of arranging for management, which is another form of psychotherapy, one needs from time to time the help of a colleague who will simply save the child from dying. Nevertheless just physically saving the life of the child does not in itself cure the anorexia which may, it is true, respond to the sort of thing that you are doing with the patients at the Central Hospital, Warwick.

In a recent case that I had in analysis it interested me very much to find, after a long period of intensive work, that the patient was not conscious of the suicidal impulse represented by the anorexia. When she became able to accept her suicidal impulses she was able to make use of the psychotherapy and we could say goodbye to the paediatricians who actually saved her life.

In a similar case at an early stage I lost a patient before my treatment had become effective because I could not find a suitable paediatric provision which would allow me to continue my work as a psychoanalyst. That was a long time ago, however, and the climate of opinion has altered.

There is still, however, this very serious propaganda by the psychiatrists who seem to be represented by Dr. Sargant and who seem to take almost anything and turn it into an illness. I feel sure you would agree that anorexia, like enuresis, is not an illness unless of course someone takes the very severe cases and gives them a label.

I hope you will not mind my writing in this way. As far as I know we never met when you were in England. I wonder what it is like practising as a psychiatrist in Western Australia.

Yours sincerely,
D. W. Winnicott, F.R.C.P.

1. William Sargant, a psychiatrist with a primarily organic orientation to mental and emotional illness.

105 ❧ To Mrs. P. Aitken

13th January 1967.

Dear Mrs. Aitken,

Thank you for writing me and for reading my book. I hope you will be able to take it that the general tendency of what I write has to do with there being no actual right and wrong. For instance, there is this matter of your husband's looking after the baby. No-one can say this is either right or wrong. Perhaps if you have several babies he will want to do this with one and not with another. The only way that babies can reach anything consistent in their environment is when the parents are able to be themselves. I do agree, however, that it is very interesting to see the effect of these details on children. For instance, he will have quite a job at some point in changing around from being maternal into being a third person in a triangle, something new. From your letter I feel fairly confident that things are going well, and certainly I do not feel a need to try to make you worry about the future.

In regard to the beginning, I wonder why you did not see the child for four days; perhaps you were exhausted. I am asking, however, because it is really terrible that really good doctors and nurses seem to be unable to leave to the mother the early stages of making a relationship. It seems to be impossible to teach doctors and nurses this one thing, that the basis of good feeding is the relationship that begins to develop between the mother and the baby. It is only too easy to imagine awful nurses and I must not jump to conclusions, but it seems to me that you could have managed the early relationship to the baby if you had been left to it and at the same time cared for properly in respect of physical nursing and doctoring. You seem to have come through this difficult phase and I hope you will be able to leave it aside now as a thing of the past. Naturally it would have been nice if all had gone well from the beginning, but at any rate for the time being you have reached some kind of equilibrium and I expect this will continue; anyhow I hope so.

It is difficult to write usefully but I hope you will at any rate not be disturbed by anything I have written. Possibly you might like to ask in the library for The Family and Individual Development (Tavistock Publications, 1965). Here you could read Chapter 13 and perhaps 14. The first two chapters might also interest you.

Yours sincerely,
D. W. Winnicott, F.R.C.P.

106 ઀ *To a Colleague*

4th September 1967.

Dear Dr. P:

I am grateful to you for sending me [your paper]. It is very rewarding for me to find that an idea of mine comes into your carefully constructed argument. I think I need not take up the points in your paper because you will know that I am in agreement with your general idea, and I feel that you have expressed yourself clearly.

Yesterday I had a patient who might have been reading your paper; a woman who has come a long way in psycho-analytic treatment and who is near to the point where she exists in such a way that she does not have to be all the time searching for herself. Referring yesterday to the illness aspect of her personality, she was describing how in an art gallery (and she is intensely interested in art) she finds herself using her body and her eyes in a search for herself. When finger-painting she is using her hands always hoping that in the result on the paper she will see herself. Everything about her in these circumstances is an instrument like a microscope being used. She is only just reaching to the position where instead of looking for herself she is able to recognise that she herself exists at the place where the search became initiated. I need not go into the reasons why she has been in this difficulty and why through the treatment she seems to be near recovering from the illness. I only mention this because it illustrates the theme of your paper and because it is fresh in my mind as a piece of clinical material.

I do hope the reception of the paper is good. Probably I shall not be able to be there as there are so many groups of meetings that many of them clash with each other. Perhaps you would be good enough to let me know how the evening goes.

Yours sincerely,
D. W. Winnicott, F.R.C.P.

107 ᛒ To Margaret Torrie

4th September 1967.

Dear Margaret Torrie:

Thank you for your letter and for the literature. I am extremely glad that you are trying to do something about the very considerable distress that goes with mastectomy. It is not at all surprising to me that you have met some fairly terrible things in response to your carefully worded questions. The paperback that you are writing should meet a real need.

I have read your preface and I have no special comment to make. No doubt in the course of the book you will be dealing with a little bit of the common pathological aspects of the problem as well as with the normal; that is to say you will be referring to the fact that a fair proportion of girls go through a period of feeling inadequate because they are not boys, and then get especially high charge of meaning in the idea of breast development so that for these a word like castration becomes appropriate when the surgeon says that the breast must come off.

The comment that I feel like making is that all women having a mastectomy must be disturbed; somewhere in every one of them is a tremendous reaction. No doubt a great deal could be done by way of preparation and sympathetic introduction to the idea. Nevertheless in my opinion nothing can really do away with their anger, hate, and sense of insult which is inherent in any mutilation even if it saves life. I think that in your writing you might somehow or other allow for the fact that the woman's anger with the callous surgeon may present some kind of an outlet for anger which otherwise eats away inside because the woman does not like to be angry with God or fate. What I am trying to say is that while I am very much in favour of an enlightened attitude towards this sort of problem and while I believe that a very great deal can be done which is not being done, nevertheless I do not expect that the problem can be solved and I do not expect you think so either. In every case the woman has to deal with resentment and there are some women who simply do not know what to do with resentment unless they can blame somebody for something. On the basis of this thought I would like to say that I think surgeons do behave in general about as badly in respect of mastectomy as they do about any of their other ploys. You could of course write an-other paperback on the management of hysterectomy and the re-moval of ovaries, etc. etc..

I do hope you will keep me in touch with what you are doing in this.

While I am writing you, may I let you know one of my own troubles? . . . It concerns the plight of . . . [a woman who] is spending more money than she has on drink. She is constantly asking me for the name of somebody who [will] help her to . . . postpone suicide . . . till her son is launched . . .

You will see my difficulty very quickly, because she cannot use me and it is difficult for me to find someone who is wise because there are not many of that kind, and she is wanting somebody who will see her without demanding a fee. I feel myself that if she got help she would be quite generous and would probably offer a present, but when a fee is demanded then she knows that she is not going to get any help. Probably this woman cannot be helped, and it is no good my recommending the local parson. If you should happen to know anyone after whose name you could put the qualification W.I.S.E., who also for some reason or other has a personal urge to help people who are in distress, I would be terribly glad if you could let me know. This person must be pre-pared to fail just as I have failed, but somehow this would seem to be very much better than what I am doing at present which is to do nothing at all simply because I don't know what to do.

I don't mind at all if you just simply ignore this part of my letter which is certainly not what you were asking for!

Every good wish to you and Alfred,

Yours,
D. W. Winnicott.

108 ᴈ☙ *To Margaret Torrie*

5th September 1967.

Dear Margaret Torrie,

One more word following my letter of yesterday. I have just read a paper by Tom Main (not published) which reviews the nature of psycho-analysis, and there is something in it which expressed an idea that I wanted to include in my letter to you yesterday. It has to do with the doctor's dilemma, by which I am not referring to Bernard Shaw's version so much as to the awkward fact that the doctor who wants to be free in his technique needs to be uninvolved emotionally. This is the quotation from Tom Main:

> "This problem—how to experience the creature of study as separate from oneself, outside oneself, different from oneself, an object of study and not a subject of experience, is far from easy. How to observe it coolly, how to record the behaviour objectively without being moved by compassion or hatred, without dread or gratitude, without distaste or sympathy, without identifying with it? These problems particularly occupy all workers who are concerned to observe and record human behaviour. Without some solution to them the surgeon (for instance) whose daily work concerns suffering, terror and pain, mutilation and death, blood and faeces and urine, could not work with cool skill. Like the biological scientist he must detach himself from the creature he deals with, defend his own objectivity, and persistently avoid any great identification with his patient's sufferings; for he has to be concerned primarily with their bodies."

I am reminded of a curious thing about myself right back in the twenties. After being an Out-patient Physician at Paddington Green I became entitled to beds. This was very exciting, because the doctor in charge of cases in the hospital has status. Having beds means that one has arrived. Hardly knowing why, I refused to step up. I got permission to use beds where necessary but I handed the in-patients over to my junior. I knew at the time why I was doing this. I said to myself: the distress of babies and small children in a hospital ward, even a very nice one, adds up to something terrific. Going into the ward disturbs me very much. If I become an in-patient doctor I shall develop the capacity not to be disturbed by the distress of the children, otherwise I shall not be able to be an effective doctor. I will therefore concentrate on my O.P. work and avoid becoming callous in order to be efficient. So I lost the status symbol but that didn't matter somehow. I think that this same thing applies to nursing, and that we have to remember it when we try to explain the extraordinary callousness which we can find in very good nurses, something which disappears when the patient is very ill physically but which becomes evident in a surprising way when the patient begins to recover physically. A special case is that of the maternity ward where the mothers and the babies are not in the category of ill unless, of course, a physical illness supervenes.

> Every good wish again,
> Yours,
> D. W. Winnicott.

109 ⧉ *To Wilfred R. Bion*

Dear Bion, 5th October 1967.

First to thank you for a very interesting evening.[1]

I am not quite settled in my mind about the idea of memory and desire or intention. When I got home Clare reminded me again that the phrase memory and desire, which you have used before, is a quotation from T. S. Eliot, and she was able to give me the whole poem, and for some reason or other I accept memory and desire as naturally interrelated in the poem. At the same time in the application of the same idea to psycho-analytic work I cannot help finding myself using the word intention and not feeling desire to be correct. As you said, we each have to find the word that fits for oneself. For me, memory and desire is all right in a poem because it refers to an experience that is 100% subjective. In the application to psycho-analytic work I find I cannot allow that this is 100% subjective. The memory includes memories of phenomena from external reality and certainly what is likely to turn up tomorrow in my analytic work cannot be covered by what I have in my own mind to want, precisely because I have to be able to allow the patient to be a separate person, as the patient has to come to be able to allow me to be outside his or her omnipotent control.

So you see why it is that I find myself unhappy with your word desire in this context.

The rest of this letter has to do with something quite separate. I am very interested in the way you bring in the Bible story in your paper on catastrophic change and also quite frequently when you are talking. I, like you, was brought up in the Christian tradition (Wesleyan) and I have no desire to throw away all that I listened to over and over again and tried to digest and sort out.

It is not possible for me to throw away religion just because the people who organize the religions of the world insist on belief in miracles. What I want to know is, have you met with the amazing book by Robert Graves and his friend Joshue Podro, called the Nazarene Gospel Restored? It is not possible to buy this book but it is in most of the libraries. Naturally it is frowned upon by all the Christian churches because it deals with the reconstruction of the Jesus story which was current but not much recorded before an attempt was made to get accepted records somewhere in the first and second centuries. In other words, by a tremendous amount of erudition and research these authors have been able to make a reconstruction of the original story, and I find a study of this book absolutely fascinating and very important for the understanding of the Bible story that we came to know so well. I wish I could buy a copy of this book and send it to you but unfortunately it is out of print.

> Every good wish,
> Yours,
> D. W. Winnicott.

1. Dr. Bion had read "Negative Capability."

110 ❧ *To Gillian Nelson*

6th October 1967.

Dear Mrs. Nelson,

Thank you for writing. There is a great deal in your letter and I cannot pretend to have properly assimilated it all yet. Everything that you say is of great interest to me. What I want to do is to try to meet your first comment.

It seems I must have failed somehow or other in Chapter 16[1] in my attempt to point out that in health the child has to come gradually to some personal method of accommodating rather than "getting rid of" aggressive feelings and impulses. I feel that in the process the child usually acts out in an aggressive way from time to time and that this is all part of life and that the mother and the father get involved and sometimes hurt. I do not mean that it seems to me good for parents to get hurt. In a sense it is their fault because on the whole they can protect themselves, but they can do this best if they know what to expect. This is rather a big subject and I do not want to spoil it by offering titbits; I would rather leave it to the imagination.

The fact does remain, however, that some parents have a problem on their hands, a child who seems to need to hurt them. There is no simple answer to this detail of management when it is a problem in the care of one child, but I suppose parents do somehow or other usually find a way of protecting themselves without reacting in such a way that the child's aggressive impulses are driven further into the unconscious so that they are liable then to appear in the form of symptoms.

I am not very pleased with this that I have written but I really wanted to write something to you in acknowledgement of your kind and interesting letter.

Yours sincerely,
D. W. Winnicott, F.R.C.P.

1. In *The Child, the Family, and the Outside World*.

111 ❧ *To Charles Clay Dahlberg*

24th October 1967.

Dear Dr. Dahlberg,

In reply to your letter of 5th October, I have lectured a great deal on the subject of physical contact between patient and therapist. If one writes these things down one gets very easily misunderstood, and I am afraid that there is no way of referring you to what I have written on this subject except to ask the reader to get a general inference from going through my writings, especially "Collected Papers: Through Paediatrics to Psycho-Analysis" (Tavistock Publications, London, 1958 and Basic Books, N.Y., 1958) and "The Maturational Processes and the Facilitating Environment" (Hogarth Press, London, 1965 and Clarke, Irwin, Toronto, 1965).

There has been a recent special occasion for discussing this over here because of the Warrendale film[1] which comes from Canada. I organized a very well-attended discussion around this film and I would like you to know that you are right in thinking that I have made a great deal of reference to this point that you are examining even if I have not written about it. I wish you well in your researches.

Yours sincerely,
D. W. Winnicott, F.R.C.P.

1. The film concerned an institution for violent children, who were physically held during attacks of violence by as many people as it took to immobilize them.

112 ❧ To Marjorie Spence

23rd November 1967.

Dear Mrs. Spence,

I am glad you wrote me because this gives us a chance to discuss together the very important matter of the way you bring up your baby. It may surprise you when I say that I cannot recognise what you seem to have found in my book.[1] Can you write again and let me know where you feel that I have made a statement like the one you refer to?[2] I would have thought that in all that I have written I have been trying to say the opposite.

In any case I feel that it is not possible to bring up a baby according to what someone says in a book. The baby has a relationship with the mother and father that develops according to what all three are like, and although it is possible to talk about what happens and to say how one thing may be better than another, the thing is how it works out naturally, and not whether it is right or wrong according to some standard statement.

It would be very good from my point of view if you could tell me that you had given over reading about these things and had allowed yourself to do what you feel and in the way you feel you would like to act both as mother and from the point of view of the baby. I did try to say in that book that the time for reading is probably after (even long after) it is all over and the children are grown up.

I very much hope I shall hear from you again.

> Yours sincerely,
> D. W. Winnicott, F.R.C.P.

1. *The Child, the Family, and the Outside World.*
2. That babies should be left to cry, even for a whole day.

113 ‽ *To Marjorie Spence*

27th November 1967.

Dear Mrs. Spence,

Thank you for your second letter. I think that you have found out a part of my book which can easily lead to misunderstanding. Perhaps the trouble comes from the fact that in my book I am not trying to tell people what to do, and of course if you have a baby in your care you are trying to get advice whenever you feel uncertain.

What I am trying to do is to draw attention to the kind of problems that do exist, and I think you may feel that I have avoided giving advice, and I do this because I feel that no two people are alike and no two babies are alike. It is only that there are certain principles that can be enunciated which apply generally.

I would have thought that it was possible to tell when a baby passes over from being angry to feeling hopeless, and I think you will find that you never want to let your child pass over this borderline. On the other hand with most small children there are quite a lot of times when the child is angry and you can see that he or she is having an experience which is real and which has to do with the fact which you refer to in your letter, that gradually a child has to meet the world and its intransigence. The mother, and the parents together, happen to be the ones who have to represent the world at this early stage.

I think that if you play for time you will find that all sorts of new things turn up which make your task easier. For instance, you will soon be able to communicate with words, and then you will find that everything becomes easier. Even being able to say "wait a minute" is a help.

I really do not feel that I have to tell you what to do, and in any case you and your husband seem to be managing very well indeed. Perhaps it would be better for you to think that your baby is telling you what babies are like much better than I could ever do in a book.

In a practical sense I suggest that it is unlikely that you will be able to prevent your baby from getting angry, although some people try to do this by meeting the child's needs in advance. Don't you think that one could carry this too far?

I do hope that I have been able to clear up the difficulty a little bit. I would be very glad if you could use my book and other books to help you to know what people think about child development and child care and not as something that can tell you what to do. In your minute-to-minute management of your baby you have to be able to be natural if you are to be consistent.

Yours sincerely,
D. W. Winnicott, F.R.C.P.

114 ⮞ *To R. S. W. Dowling*

8th December 1967.

Dear Dr. Dowling,

I am grateful to you for the invitation contained in your letter of 24th November. It is possible that I will not be able to do what you suggest because I am so fully occupied at the present moment.

I want you to consider another point while you are at it. There cannot be a chapter on the child's mind as if the mind were just like something like the child's liver or the child's blood. The child is a total personality in process of growth and there is no possibility of a statement about the developing human personality except a long one occupying many volumes. It simply cannot be tagged on to a book about napkin rashes and where to get a good cot!

I think perhaps you can see that I am reluctant to be associated with the idea of writing a bit about the child's mind to be inserted in your perfectly good book on the child's functioning body. Of course I may be wrong, and you may find some very good person to write a valuable chapter or two about some aspect of a child's behaviour, or of the things that make for happiness. It would be very bad, however, for me to associate myself with the idea of a bit about the person in a book about bodies looked at from the medical angle which concerns itself with health as the absence of diseases.

I like your book as it is, and I think it has real value, and it would be very easy for you to spoil it by tagging on a little bit about a subject which is really bigger even than the subject of the functioning of the body and everything that the paediatrician stands for.

I wonder if you perhaps don't agree with me. What about taking this letter and showing it to somebody like Dr. Hersov who is at Great Ormond Street, or Dr. Heinz Wolff of the Maudsley, or perhaps John Bowlby? I believe quite an important principle is involved and particularly I think in the type of presentation that is needed when discussion is about the developing human being. For instance, the first thing would be to cut out all advertisements; and the second thing would be to cut out the idea of universal dissemination, and substitute the idea of something that is available on application. What I mean is that when people want to know something about what is happening when they see a new human being starting to develop, the matter can be discussed with them, but it is an intrusion to put across this kind of thing to people who have not asked for it.

Yours sincerely,
D. W. Winnicott, F.R.C.P.

115 ⧫ *To Donald Gough*

6th March 1968.

Dear Dr. Gough,

I am sure you don't want this back but I am sending it to you because I thought I would like to write in any case. I hope that you felt that I gave the Medical Section meeting proper publicity.

I want to let you know that you have done something quite important for me in drawing attention to the interaction through the eyes which accompanies feeding in the first weeks. What I have learned has enabled me to step up my use of direct confrontation at certain phases in certain analyses and has had a material effect also on my conceptualization of early relationships. In due course all these things will bear fruit if we live long enough. Meanwhile you will go ahead with drawing our attention to facts. I love to think of all the clinical observations that are waiting for us to make but it is a question of he who hath eyes to see let him hear!

Sometime I want to use what you have shown us in this way, that in using the breast (or bottle) the baby is experimenting in exteriorizing the object, which interferes with the state of being merged in with the mother which obtains as a primary state. The interaction through the eyes seems to me to be holding on to the merging which may very likely facilitate the experiments in the exteriorization of the object. I don't know how to put it better at the present moment.

I would even go on to say that when looking becomes equated with feeding, as when we read, then we begin to want something else to do for us what the eye business does for us when in the original feeding situation. For instance, we might want to smoke. There are all sorts of possibilities here which are simply just fun unless one is engaged in a treatment where these matters may make all the difference between success and failure at a crucial stage of an analysis.

You will see that I am letting you know how much I appreciate what you are teaching us and the sort of limited observations which you can bring forward for us to consider by means of the work you put into filming.

I hope the Medical Section meeting will be a success. I shall not be able to be present as far as I can see.

> Yours,
> D. W. Winnicott, F.R.C.P.

116 ᶲ *To L. Joseph Stone*

18th June 1968.

Dear Mr. Stone,

Thank you for writing me. The case that I gave at the A.C.P.P. was descriptive and not committed to paper. There are now several references to the Squiggle Game in published cases[1] and I would like to refer you to the following:—

"A Child Psychiatry Case Illustrating Delayed Reaction to Loss." In: Drives, Affects, Behavior, Ed. Max Schur, Int. Univ. Press, Inc., N.Y. 1965. (Reprint enclosed.)

"Child Therapy: A Case of Antisocial Behaviour." In: Modern Perspectives in Child Psychiatry. Ed. John G. Howells. Oliver & Boyd, London, 1965. (No reprints available).

"A Psychoanalytic View of the Antisocial Tendency." In: Crime, Law and Corrections. Ed. Ralph Slovenko. Charles C. Thomas, Springfield, Illinois, 1966. (Reprint enclosed).

"The Value of the Therapeutic Consultation." In: Foundations of Child Psychiatry. Ed. Emanuel Miller, Pergamon Press, London, 1968. (No reprints available).

You may remember there was also one case briefly described in my Collected Papers: Through Paediatrics to Psycho-Analysis (Chapter 9).

A further account will appear in "Voices" published in Atlanta by John Warkentin, but this is not yet out.

There are others but I think they are unlikely to add anything significant to your understanding.

The one that is most easy to reach from your point of view is "A Clinical Study of the Effect of a Failure of the Average Expectable Environment on a Child's Mental Functioning" and I enclose a reprint of this.

I do intend to gather all these ideas together but you can imagine how reluctant I am to start up a "squiggle technique" as a rival to other projection techniques. It would defeat the main object of the exercise if something stereotyped were to emerge like the Rorschach test. Essential is the absolute freedom so that any modification may be accepted if appropriate. Perhaps a distinctive feature is not the use of drawings so much as the free participation of the analyst acting as psycho-therapist.

I love to talk about these things illustrating the use of the squiggles by reference to therapeutic consultation examples, but at the same time, as I hope you can see, I am very reluctant to put it down once and for all on paper. I would rather that each worker in the field should evolve his own method as I evolved mine.

I hope to be in New York in November and perhaps we may have a chance to meet then and to discuss the matter, and in fact I shall be giving some cases at the William Alanson White Institute (November 8th).

Yours very sincerely,
D. W. Winnicott, F.R.C.P.

1. All the cases mentioned, except the first, are in *Therapeutic Consultations in Child Psychiatry* (New York: Basic Books, 1971). The first will appear in *Psychoanalytic Explorations,* a forthcoming two-volume collection of previously unpublished writings of Winnicott.

117 ❧ *To Adam Limentani*

27th September 1968.

Dear Limentani,

I guess you found it rather a waste of time at the 1952 Club the other evening.[1] From my point of view I did learn something in the second half, after the interval. I seem to be unable to pull it off when I visit the '52 Club which is a pity because it provides a good opportunity for an easy discussion.

Incidentally, I would like to say that I know that my three talks every year to the students are likely to produce a certain amount of upheaval. I would like to make a comment. Firstly, as I believe you understand, I am not trying to cause an upheaval; but I do find the students remarkably frightened into conformity. This year this was less true than usual. There is hardly any reaction during the discussion when I talk to students that is comparable at all to the reactions that the analysts of these students get during the next week. I suppose all this is inevitable. I do worry, however, on the score that students seem to be taught that psycho-analysis of what is called orthodox variety is something that can be counted on to be successful in the end if you plod on. On the whole the students do not seem to have been told that all analysts fail and that they all have difficult cases and that they all want new developments in theory which will widen the scope and make possible the treatment of less carefully chosen cases.

The other thing I want to say is this. It is not really a good idea for someone with my experience to talk three times to a group of students. What can I do? I can hide all my discontent and I can add a little bit more to the complacency which I find around me, or alternatively I can let the students know some of the difficulties which will arise in their practices quite soon inevitably. There is nothing in between these two extremes because in three times one cannot develop gradually the exposition of a point of view. I do realise very well indeed from having been Training Secretary that there is not enough student-time for you to be able to ask senior analysts to give long courses of either lectures or seminars. This is part of the facts of life. Nevertheless I do feel that Dr. Balint was right when he said that he would not speak to students three times. The only reason why I continue to consent when invited is that I am afraid that otherwise I will never see the students at all.

I could add an historical detail. For a long time, as you know, I was not asked to do any teaching of psycho-analysis because neither Miss Freud nor Mrs. Klein would use me or allow their students to come to me for regular teaching even in child analysis. I therefore missed at a critical time in my life the stimulus which would have made me work up a lecture series definitely orientated to the teaching of technique. When later on I became acceptable and was invited to do some teaching, I had already had some original ideas and naturally these came to mind when I was planning to talk to the students. This accounts to some extent for the way things are. I am not complaining, only I think that these matters of history are sometimes interesting.

With good wishes,
Yours,
D. W. Winnicott, F.R.C.P.

1. The 1952 Club is a small association of distinguished British psychoanalysts.

118 ᵉ᎒ *To F. Robert Rodman*

10th January 1969.

Dear Dr. Rodman,

I have now had time to read your paper on *Accidental Technical Lapses as Therapy.* I find these notes very interesting and I hope that you will continue your attempt to bring these views together in the form of a contribution for publication.

It is quite a difficult subject in the sense that one can so easily be misunderstood, and obviously it is much easier to pretend that there is some kind of perfection of technique which can be taught and acquired than to acknowledge the mistakes one makes and then to go further and to see whether sometimes these mistakes have value. I fully agree with this last idea and I think you know that various examples, sometimes rather terrible ones, are scattered throughout my later writings. Certainly I have been guilty of startling senior students by telling them about technical mistakes, some of which turn out to be valuable, and offering them for discussion. Actually students do not like this sort of thing, because, as you describe, they are trying to organize themselves on the basis of choosing identifications, and they are not ready yet to deal with personal idiosyncrasies. What I feel that you leave out in your paper is a clear statement that diagnosis matters. For instance, I think that mistakes may be dangerous in the analysis of psychoneurosis while at the same time they may be useful when the patient is more psychotic or what we call borderline. I think myself that the difference is that the neurotic, if there is such a thing as a purely neurotic, is not only able to deal with an analysis in terms of verbalization, but also he or she takes for granted all the stuff that is being worked over in the analysis of a borderline case, most of which is preverbal. In other words, in the extreme of a borderline case everything boils down in the end to what I have tried to describe as the survival of the analyst, only it may take years for the patient to become sufficiently confident in the transference to be able to take the risk of a relationship in which the analyst is absolutely unprotected. I have just read a paper on this to the New York Psychoanalytic Society but my ideas are not well formulated in this paper. The idea is there, however, that when the patient gets towards this very serious state of affairs then almost anything can happen and it is irrelevant. The only thing is arriving at the point at which the risk is taken and the analyst survives or does not survive.

(I know the wording is wrong here. It is not just a question of survival but it is a question of surviving without change into re-taliation.)

All this leads on to the thing that we are always saying which is that we want to choose for students patients who are not border-line and who will not have false selves and who are psychoneurotic and who will play the game of a verbalized psycho-analysis as invented by Freud. It is only on such material that the students can learn psycho-analysis. When they have become proficient in this and have come to trust their own belief in their basic identifica-tions (with analysts) they can start meeting not the patient's in-stinctual desires but the patient's basic needs. In other words, they can start trying to treat borderline patients and a false-self organi-zation where, as it were, a nursemaid brings the patient for anal-ysis.

The analyst must be temperamentally suited for this kind of deeper work which is not always successful in terms of cure. If the patient feels that it is worth doing, it is worth doing, in spite of the fact that every stage which could be called an advance brings the patient into closer contact with pain. In other words, the pa-tient gives up defences, and the pain is always there against which the defences were organized. This kind of work, as I have pointed out in talking about the treatment of psychotic children, could be described as cruel. When it succeeds, of course, the cruelty and the suffering are forgotten.

There is one kind of mistake that I would like to mention. With patients who must have a period of regression to dependence so that for many weeks, even months, one is on one's best behaviour and the strain can be terrific, there comes a moment when the need for such careful adaptation to need is lessened. With me, at this point I tend to misbehave; as a patient of mine told me when trying to educate me, 'If I give you an inch you take an ell.' In other words, the relief that comes from not having to be so artificially adaptive, quite beyond what I will do in private life, is so great that I begin to swallow the bait that the patient offers and find myself talking about things in general and acting as if the patient had suddenly become well. This is a very great danger area in the treatment of borderline cases where regression to dependence is a prominent feature. Perhaps you would agree with this. On the other hand I do not want to say that even this kind of mistake is quite useless if the case survives the experience. Undoubtedly it does then show the patient to what an extent one was under strain. The awful thing when a patient commits suicide at this stage is that this leaves the analyst for ever holding the strain and never able to misbehave just a little. I think that this is an inherent part of the revenge that suicide of this kind contains, and I must say that the analyst always deserves what he gets here. I say this having just lost a patient through being ill. I could not help being ill, but if I am going to be ill then I must not take on this kind of patient. It is almost mechanistic when we think how things work in this area.

I do hope you will continue your work and keep me informed.

Yours sincerely,
D. W. Winnicott, F.R.C.P.

119 ❧ *To an American Correspondent*

14th January 1969.

Dear Mr. Q:

Your letter reached me about six months ago, but a great deal has happened here since then. Not only was I not too well myself, but also I visited New York, and there became very ill for some weeks. I am now convalescent from this illness and that is why I have had time at last to settle down to reading your letter. Of course one can always read a letter through, but that was no good with your letter because in it you ask questions and raise problems that are at the edge of our understanding. It must have seemed "forever" that I have delayed answering, but here at least I am acknowledging your letter, and I may be able to venture some kind of a comment.

I am so glad that you found my attempt to state and to understand your kind of problem encouraging, and a little useful perhaps. You might find more help in a more recent book of mine: The Maturational Processes and the Facilitating Environment. (Hogarth Press, London, 1965)—a volume in the International Psycho-analytic Library.

May I refer to the places where I speak of the *unthinkable anxiety* that some people have to carry round with them all their lives. My use of the word "unthinkable" might provide a link with your disappearing mind which you closely associate with the core of yourself. (In the book you refer to I wrote of a split-off intellect which bothers some people but this isn't just what you are referring to; you are talking about a loss of your capacity to be a whole integrated human being, containing and able to stand (tolerate) whatever anxieties (and good things) may be in your total make-up.)

It could be that if you are "all there" then sooner or later this anxiety beyond what you can tolerate comes over you, and you cannot hold it long enough to look at it and see what is the content of the anxiety. If you could do this you would find that it contains—at root—the deepest source of your own psychic energy, so that when you have to blot it out (or it happens to you that it gets blotted out) you lose the taproot, so to speak.

Now when I have had the chance to try to help individual patients in this sort of trouble I have had to provide an environment for them that gets very near to the state of affairs that usually obtains when a mother has a baby of her own, at the start. The mother is for the time being totally committed to the task of adaptation to the infant's needs,—living, for instance, in the baby's time, not in her own, etc. etc.

It is very difficult to do this in a treatment and I often have failed to do it well enough, or have faltered at a critical moment. It is a cruel thing to try to do because success is so precarious, and every failure unthinkably painful to the patient.

The healing comes when trust in the "mother" is so great that the patient can be angry at the least sign of failure of adaptation. In this way the patient gets back to the anger that would have been appropriate at the earliest stage.

Now we can guess at your mother's failure, in that at some point she failed (I'm sorry for her) to protect you from a father as you describe him. So at some point, before you had managed to get to a love of him which would allow you *also* to hate him, he showed hate of you, and so you lost your own destructive murderous hate which in any case by then was only rudimentary. (I have to do the guessing here.) So for your own basic aggression you had to rely on its turning up in the shape of your father's "mad" aggressiveness. Your brother seems to have been the same, but (as you describe it) he tried to regain his *own* aggression by becoming a "good" destructive U.S.A. soldier; the price being his own death.

Can you see that if you had been able to reach your own aggression you could have found that the world in fact survives, and then you could have had a look at your aggressiveness and found that it provides one of the roots of living energy? There is also love, in the more bodily sense, leading up to sexuality and genitality and object love, but so much of life does consist in constructive activity that has as its back-cloth the total of aggressive and destructive fantasy.

I am not expecting you to be able to get my full meaning, but all I can do is to try to understand you a little, because I am not able to provide conditions in which you could reach to the initial trustfulness that you inherited, out of which you were rudely and prematurely shaken, because of mother's timidity plus father's wild outbursts.

You should know that these problems assail everyone to some extent, but for you the reality of your parents' state planted a pattern on your condition and made it impossible for you to provide for yourself the facilitating environment that would allow your maturational processes to take effect.

> I send you my greetings.
> Yours sincerely,
> D. W. Winnicott, F.R.C.P.

120 ⮰ *To Anna Freud*

20th January 1969.

Dear Anna Freud:

I am grateful to you for your letter which you wrote concerning my illness.[1] Now I am convalescent at home all seems well, but I cannot yet plan for my future professionally.

While I am writing I want to let you know how sorry I am that your brother Ernst has been ill again.

If you were to ask me what about my paper, The Use of an Object, I would say that the answer is complex. I read the paper and got considerable personal benefit from the reaction of the three discussants, so that I am now in process of rewriting it in a quite different language. The unfortunate thing was that the three said discussants occupied the whole of the time so that there could be no response from the very large audience which collected for some reason unspecified. There was an internal TV arranged so that the overflow in the library could watch me, which I thought rather amusing. Actually I was already ill but I think this was not noticed.

> With good wishes,
> Yours very sincerely,
> D. W. Winnicott, F.R.C.P.

1. Winnicott had been stricken with Asian influenza while visiting New York to present "The Use of an Object" to the New York Psychoanalytic Society. He developed pulmonary edema and was close to death for some time.

121 ⮞ *To J. D. Collinson*

10th March 1969.

Dear Mr. Collinson,

I was very glad to hear from you from the centre of Tanzania, and it is fun for me to think that my book has reached Tabora. My greetings to your wife and to yourself and I hope that your ex-2-year-old is developing well.

It does not surprise me at all that you see some sort of connection between social anthropology and a study of babyhood, especially if babyhood is taken to include the dependence which is part of it. Perhaps some time or other I shall be able to read your article on universals of symbolism.

It is difficult to answer your very interesting questions in a letter. We need to meet and to discuss the ideas that we have in common and the places where we may find ourselves disagreeing. From my point of view, *innate* leaves it open more than the word *inborn* would do, for a concept of tendencies as inherited but not necessarily reached. I called one of my books *The Maturational Processes and the Facilitating Environment* and you can see from this title that I find the inherited tendency cannot operate alone, and that in the developing baby and child it is the environment that facilitates individual growth. The opposite extreme would be to say that we teach our children everything, which of course is manifestly absurd. We cannot even teach them to walk, but their innate tendency to walk at a certain age needs us as supporting figures, and quite possibly your own child needed to touch somebody's finger while walking at an early stage, getting moral support for something which had already become a possibility for him or her in physiological and anatomical terms. I think you will find that it will not be difficult for us to agree in these matters but of course my use of words may pull red herrings across issues which, if better stated, would be quite simple.

In regard to the more difficult question of morality, I do feel that the same principles that I have just been discussing apply, but of course the whole thing is very much more complex. I could not say that I think that the principles of right and wrong are inborn. Nevertheless I believe that they cannot be taught; or that if they can be taught they are not very useful. In between is the idea that babies and children come to some kind of personal morality in so far as they have found themselves and have begun to have a sense of personal existence and self-knowledge. It has to be very complicated, and it is no use my trying to make it sound simple, and here again I am sure I will have your agreement.

While the processes of development are making headway in the individual child in what I call the facilitating environment, the child is able to find temporary solutions in terms of identifications, to be like mother or father or someone else in the surroundings. On the other hand, morality in the end must be a personal morality and not one that is simply taken over from the parent-figures; that is to say in health. One cannot assume that all children are fully healthy in the psychiatric sense, and surely in any family one must expect to find not only all kinds of children, but all stages of health and ill-health, of the kind that we are discussing.

Referring to the end of your second paragraph, I think the word *innate* can carry the idea not only of inherited tendencies towards basic impulses, but also the tendencies towards growth of all kinds, growth which perhaps does not have any meaning, in early childhood, but becomes meaningful at a later stage. This is particularly clearly shown in terms of adolescent growth. Also the inherited tendency towards integration of the personality may be the most important inherited thing in human beings, and this touches on the whole subject of what the psycho-analysts refer to as ego psychology and the work that has been done chiefly by psychoanalysts in the last two decades, that is to say, since Freud died.

Reading your letter I feel that if we were having a conversation we could very easily agree about these matters, yet how difficult they are to state in terms that have universal significance. I shall send this letter so that you get a reply quickly, but I would like to put you in touch with other literature perhaps not easily available where you are situated. There are other books of my own which follow up the ideas in the Pelican, and I would gladly send you copies of these books. It must be very difficult, living so far away from the home country, to know what of the thousands of books that are published might be valuable to order from a book-seller.

I shall expect, then, to hear from you if you wish me to send you either the names of books or else the books themselves.

> With good wishes,
> Yours sincerely,
> D. W. Winnicott, F.R.C.P.

122 ❧ *To M. B. Conran*

8th May 1969.

Dear Dr. Conran,

You will have had a preliminary note from me soon after March 19th when you wrote me. In this note I said no more than that I valued being used, and survived what you called a flood unleased. Often since then I have thought of trying to make a further comment on your letter, or at any rate trying to learn something from what you have written in it. It seems that until today I have not really properly absorbed the contents of your letter. It would be, fun if we could easily meet and talk these things over, but I think that for both of us this is truly difficult to arrange. We could, however, try. As for myself, I have at present the perfect excuse— someone has stolen my car!

Let me first make a comment on the third paragraph of your first page, if you still have a carbon of it to which you can refer. I tend to agree with your description of the child taking medicine completely innocent of pharmacology and only knowing about the mother's attitude. In some way or other medicine must be nasty. When I was seeing a vast number of mothers and small children I discovered that a lot of what we did to make medicine nice was wasted effort and seemed to the child to be part of a grand deception. We had one very good way of getting round this and that was to invent a food, such as Parrishes Food, which could be joined up with Cod Liver Oil & Malt. This now became a pana- cea, not only being good for slum children brought up in the dark, but also accepted as a food that you get at hospital. It did not, however, alter the general principle that medicine is nasty. I would go so far as to say that we had a category of patient, rather a common patient, who liked nasty medicine and craved for it, and in the extreme preferred it to food. This was a kind of inverted anorexia. Often this fitted in with something in the mother, but not always, as it could be an inconvenient management detail adding to the task of the normal mother. I got to know a lot about all this in the first 25 years of my paediatric practice when of course we always gave one, two, or three bottles of something or other, or pills, to every patient. Eventually I dropped the whole thing and dropped prescribing altogether; but this of course meant that I had to deal with the patients in a much more personal way and I had lost the short-cut to happiness or to psycho-therapy. I had at the same time aligned myself better to the intelligence and the growing understanding based on education of the East and North Kensington slum mothers.

I give all these details to let you know that I am aware of the problems that you touch on in this paragraph about medicines, and I know that it has a direct significance when one comes to consider psychiatric medication in terms of tranquillisers, sleeping draughts, anti-depressants, and drugs that are supposed to cure schizophrenia. (I see in the popular press that a new drug is to be given to the lucky doctors in Dublin or somewhere next week which enables schizophrenia to be treated at home!)

It seemed to me to be logical for you to go on in your writing to a description of the Charge Nurses and their personalities and temperaments; and then you come to R. You certainly have problems! It was remarkable the way that he eventually discharged himself and went home. His return and the very dangerous position that you got into reminds me that I was greatly helped in my hospital practice (even dealing only with children) when I invented the diagnosis: "Children that I cannot help." I cannot see why it is that we should imagine we can successfully treat every case when, apart from heredity, there can be such a long history of mismanagement that there is too much to counteract, and also when these patients become hopeful they need to test us out more than we can perhaps stand. You will agree with me, I think, that the only satisfactory thing you can do for a patient who is violent in the way that R was violent on that particular day is to survive and to go through the experience without the patient detecting a retaliatory element in our attitude. I think you were in danger here of not surviving, or at any rate of becoming damaged, and certainly the patient cannot derive benefit from having done damage to you or to any of your staff or perhaps even to the building. I acknowledge that the building has to suffer to some extent, and perhaps the casual observer would say that the building suffers a great deal, but it can be mended. The limit of the damage to a human being seems to me to be measured in terms of exhaustion rather than damage. Damage cannot ever be helpful to the patient, and patients when they do damage are always very near to suicide. I am putting this dogmatically, and probably it will be very obvious to you that what I am saying is true, or else you will let me know where you feel that I am wrong.

The trouble now comes from your inability to find staff who can give you support exactly along the lines that you can just manage to act yourself. I can well see that the Villa must fail sometimes in regard to its two principles. Sometimes one has to transfer a patient in analysis to a mental hospital, and for the time being abandon the taking of responsibility for the case, and certainly a lot of my patients at any rate go to their doctor or chemist for drugs. I very seldom hand out drugs myself but then of course there is a very distinct limit to the degree of illness which I can accept in my kind of practice. There are immense difficulties when we try to co-operate with a General Practitioner, for instance, in the matter of drugs, and the difficulties come from the patient who is dissociated and who necessarily plays one doctor against another, so that I and my friend the G.P. collude with opposite elements in the dissociation of the patient and when we meet socially we hardly recognize each other unless we can see the funny side of it and laugh.

On page three at the top I can see that S was at the end of his tether. It is because of the sort of feelings that S was describing here that I wrote a chapter of my book called "Hate in the Countertransference." I felt that it was necessary for us to fully acknowledge the moments at which the behavior of a patient is intolerable to a particular doctor or nurse for one reason or another. As you more or less say, there is a very great deal of difference between hatred and retaliation developing in one's attitude. There are times when a patient can feel relieved when told that he is hated but if we are to do this the patient must be well enough to listen to the words, and this of course may not be in the picture.

I am now in the middle of page three. It must be very distressing when you find complaints being made above your head by your staff members. Your own latent paranoia (and I have plenty myself) becomes roused after a bit. You had a very good example here of R exploiting one side against another in the total staff situation. From his point of view survival of the Villa meant nothing unless he had done everything in his power to make it smash itself up from inside. It is very interesting indeed that S's behaviour moderated when you brought these things out into the open.

Then the question arises, what about drugs? because everyone has got to the end of what can be stood, and so the drugs get stepped up and you are back in routine psychiatric practice.

I have not so far referred to the complication of S's mother who seemed to have a necessity to prove you to be human and imperfect. Then it seems that S himself began to criticize you for having gone against your principles, and you find yourself supporting your nurses as people rather than principles which are dead things although they can become of vital significance. The outcome was (at the time you wrote) that S was not being given drugs and you began to find him less ugly. I suppose ugly here means provocative, provoking ugly reactions. Released from this you find yourselves being fond of each other, or should I say loving each other; and then you have to deal with love turning up unexpectedly and the complications that belong to this unexpected feature. It is most interesting the way in which you sum up at the end by saying that the affective (or perhaps you mean effective) component of the interpretation was clearly experienced by the nurse, that is to say, not by S. In other words the mother had eaten grapes that were not sour and it was the child's teeth that ceased to be set on edge.

You may or may not find this letter useful but perhaps you can find it entertaining. At any rate I hope you will see that I enjoyed your communication.

> With good wishes,
> Yours very sincerely,
> D. W. Winnicott, F.R.C.P.

123 ⮞ *To Agnes Wilkinson*

9th June 1969.

Dear Dr. Wilkinson,

Thank you so much for writing me.

It is interesting, what you say about intellectual honesty. I remember as I was putting this in I thought to myself "really it is only in the split-off intellect that one can be 100% honest; as soon as living processes come in, then there is self-deception and deception and compromise and ambivalence."

As for T, it would be very interesting for me to have a talk with him, but I cannot imagine being able to give him valuable ideas or a new slant on this vexed problem.

Incidentally, there is my lecture to the Newcastle Conference of the Student Health Association, a proof of which was not sent me, and I hate to think of its going out under my name. I could let you have an offprint of a corrected version of this should you want it, but I know of course that this lecture, although it meant quite a lot to me myself, did not get to the heart of the matter. I don't suppose anyone can get to the heart of the matter like this, but at the same time one has to admit that there are problems of management which belong to the here and now, and that are separate from matters of eternal truth. It's fun to hear from you.

Yours,
D. W. Winnicott, F.R.C.P.

124 ⮞ *To William W. Sargant*

24th June 1969.

Dear Dr. Sargant,

You may be surprised to hear from me out of the blue, but there is a communication I want to make, and the stimulus is your interesting article on *The Physiology of Faith* in World Medicine.

When we meet you always seem to be friendly and we seem to get on all right together, and you did indeed say some words to Robert Graves which made him think that I was not altogether reprehensible. Can you accept, therefore, a letter from me in which I express some criticism?

In this article to which I refer, as in so many of the things you write, you take the trouble to inject something about psycho-analysis in the sort of way that has an effect on readers perhaps greater than that of the article itself. The readers find themselves caught up in your general argument and descriptive writing, and they do not bother to question the two or three things that you let drop, so that it amounts to a kind of propaganda against something that you call psycho-analysis.

In this article you will recognise what I am saying if you look at page 19 in the middle of the first paragraph. You jump from Buddha and Christ to Freud and Jung, and the uninformed reader simply takes it for granted that on the couch the patient is being invited in a more or less subtle way to acquire absolute faith. This joins up with a shorter reference on page 14: ". . . . such as the psycho-analyst's absolute and unshakeable faith in the existence of a highly sexualized Freudian subconscious mind;. . . ." I suggest that you are letting yourself down very badly when you continuously do this sort of thing.

I have to ask myself where it was that you became acquainted with psycho-analysis and analytic psychology. I of course know analysts who are dogmatic and indoctrinating types and from my point of view they are all bad analysts. What I know of Jungians makes me feel the same way about them, that when they work on the basis of the sort of belief in Jung that you are referring to, they are bad Jungians. Perhaps you became acquainted with psycho-analysis by reading certain statements of Freud belonging to the first twenty years of this century when he was working away at his attempt to build on the basis of his theory which was already pretty well stated in *The Interpretation of Dreams* in 1900.

For my part, coming into psycho-analysis in the early twenties, and having an analysis by James Strachey (who was certainly not blinded by any kind of faith) I have not found psycho-analysis to be at all like what you describe. I think growing up in the psycho-analytic group and knowing all its internal strains and stresses, I only know of psycho-analysis as a struggling science, and certainly as I never knew Freud I never came to a faith in him that you are always talking about. I had my early loyalties to Freud, to Melanie Klein, and to others, but eventually the loyalty is to oneself, and this must be true of most of my colleagues. I really do believe that you have got stuck in your view of dynamic psychology somewhere right back three or four decades ago and I think it is a great pity.

I could go further and make a comment that there seems to be no playing in what you write and therefore a lack of creativity. Perhaps you reserve your creativity for some other part of your life, in friendships for instance, or in painting. I don't know. The result, however, as comes over rather well in this shortened version of your Maudsley Lecture, is a materialism of a gross kind, and the only good thing that I can see from it is that it gives us a close view of the way the next dictator will work, and maybe it is we who will be the victims and for whom the dictator will make life not worth living because of the destruction of personal creative living at its root.

In other words, if I thought of you as personally represented in this article, I would feel that you and I could never meet again as two human beings even if we were to talk together. This is what is mysterious for me, because when I meet you I find that I am talking to another human being, a sensitive person and one who really cares about his patients.

In terms of faith it seems to me that what you write in this article leaves out faith in biology and its processes which have flowered in matters of human personality and human inter-relationships and the summation of human achievement, usually referred to by the terms civilization and culture.

When I look round to try to find why it is that I have written you in this way just at this moment I cannot answer the question that I ask myself.

Sincerely yours,
D. W. Winnicott, F.R.C.P.

125 ᴥ *To Helm Stierlin*

31st July 1969.

Dear Dr. Stierlin,

I am grateful to you for sending me a copy of *Conflict and Reconciliation*. I can see that you have tried to give a comprehensive view of the basis for schizophrenia in its human relations aspect. As you know, I have a great interest in this field.

I am taking the opportunity to send you a reprint of something which quite likely you have already met (La Schizophréne Infantile en Termes d'Echec d'Adaptation).

I have not read your book through, as I hope I shall do. At this moment what I would like to do is to say that in the quotation you kindly make, page 87, from my writings, *you* use the words *good experience*. It is important to me that in my writings I always say *good-enough* rather than *good*. I think that the words *good-enough* help to steer the reader away from sentimentality and idealisation. Incidentally, you list me in the index as being quoted on page 78, which is wrong by one line because somehow or other my name has got pushed over, perhaps by the printer, to page 79; A very small detail indeed. I am grateful to you for referring in this way to my writings.

Should you be going into another edition, you could put under my name in the selected bibliography the names of the books instead of the papers, which people often find it difficult to get in touch with.

Incidentally, *Mother and Child: A Primer of First Relationships* has been withdrawn, and the English version is now available in U.S.A., a Penguin (*Pelican A668*).

The other three references could be better given as:

(1) Collected Papers: Through Paediatrics to Psycho-Analysis. Tavistock Publications, London, 1958.
(2) The Family and Individual Development. Tavistock Publications, London, 1965.
(3) The Maturational Processes and the Facilitating Environment. Hogarth Press, London, 1965.

All these details are relatively unimportant, but perhaps you can hand this letter to the proper quarter and in another edition use my suggestions.

I hope the book will go well, and I expect to write you again in a month or two.

Yours very sincerely,
D. W. Winnicott, F.R.C.P.

126 ⮂ To Robert Tod

6th November 1969.

Dear Robert,

I hardly know how to answer your letter of 30th October. I think you have had the main things about my life in so far as they are fit to publish.

I became a Physician in charge of my own Department at the Paddington Green Children's Hospital in 1923 and retired after 40 years. In the course of that time there was a gradual shift in the work of the Department from physical illness to emotional disturbance or to the psychological aspect of the personality if one uses the word psychological without specifically linking it with academic psychology.

At the same time I had an appointment of a similar nature in the decade 1923/33 in the East End at the Queen's Hospital for Children, now Queen Elizabeth's. Here I saw a very large number of patients and was in charge of the L[ondon] C[ounty] C[ouncil] Rheumatism Clinic which dealt with rheumatic fever and chorea and concomitant heart disease. Mercifully this physical syndrome died out in the mid-thirties.

I also had experience in the early twenties of some other very bad epidemics, notably encephalitis lethargica. We also had to deal with very severe summer diarrhoea and various polio epidemics, and of course those were the days before antibotics, so that our wards were full of children with pus in the lungs or the bones or the meninges. Penicillin put a stop to all that and transformed physical paediatrics into something which could afford to look at the disturbances that belong to the lives of children who are physically healthy. In a way, therefore, the advances of physical paediatrics opened up the field for child psychiatry. I tried to make full use of this new development.

In the way I became involved with the failures of the evacuation scheme and I could therefore no longer avoid the subject of the antisocial tendency. Eventually I became interested in the etiology of delinquency and therefore joined up quite naturally with John Bowlby who at that time was starting up his work based on the relationship that he observed between delinquency and periods of separation at significant times in the child's early life.

I cannot imagine what you can get out of all this for your biographical note.

All the time, starting right back in 1923 when I started my own personal analysis, I have been involved with psycho-analysis, becoming a student at the Institute for Psycho-Analysis in the late twenties, and a qualified analyst in the early thirties. For about 10 years I did child analysis in a concentrated way. After the war, however, I kept up my psycho-analytic work more in terms of adults and later on I came to deal with adolescents. Somehow or other after holding various posts in the British Psycho-Analytical Society I became President, and I have had two periods in which I have served as President for three years.

Now I am engaged in developing my technique for dealing with the private cases, which has special features and whose chief characteristic is that oneself is the whole team and oneself takes total responsibility. As can be guessed, there are advantages here as well as disadvantages.

Probably this is not all what you want to know but how else can I try to help you? Ring me up if you want to discuss it.

> Good wishes,
> Yours sincerely,
> D. W. Winnicott, F.R.C.P.

Winnicott's Correspondents

CONRAN, M. B.
Psychiatric Registrar, Shenley Hospital, St. Albans; Associate member, BPS.

DAHLBERG, CHARLES CLAY
Research psychologist, William Alanson White Institute of Psychiatry, New York City.

DOWLING, R. S. W.
Editor of the periodical *Family Doctor*.

EZRIEL, H.
Associate member, BPS.

FEDERN, PAUL
Early contributor to the psychoanalytic literature on psychosis.

FITZGERALD, OTHO W.S.
Medical superintendent at Shenley Hospital, St. Albans.

FORDHAM, MICHAEL
Jungian analyst; friend of Winnicott's.

FRANK, KLARA
Member, BPS; associate of Anna Freud.

FREUD, ANNA
Daughter of Sigmund Freud; one of the founders of child psychoanalysis; prolific author; founder of the Hampstead Child-Therapy Course and Clinic.

FRIEDLANDER, KATE
Member, BPS; associate of Anna Freud.

GLOVER, EDWARD
Controversial member of the BPS who resigned in the 1940s; ardent opponent of the ideas of Melanie Klein.

GOUGH, DONALD
Associate member, BPS; consultant psychiatrist to National Spastics Society; Child psychiatrist.

GUNTRIP, HARRY
Formerly a minister; psychoanalyst; analysand of Fairbairn and Winnicott; originator of a theory of the origin and treatment of schizoid phenomena.

HAZLEHURST, R. S.
Minister who responded to Winnicott's letter to the *Times* (Letter 12).

HENDERSON, SIR DAVID K.
Professor of psychiatry, Edinburgh University; consultant psychiatrist, Royal Infirmary, Edinburgh.

HODGE, S. H.
Minister who responded to Winnicott's letter to the *Times* (Letter 12).

HOFFER, WILLI
Member, BPS; associate of Anna Freud.

JAMES, MARTIN
Member, BPS; friend of Winnicott's; one of the Middle Group.

JAQUES, ELLIOT
Member, BPS; writer on the subject of "mid-life crisis."

JONES, ERNEST
One of Freud's earliest circle; biographer of Freud; instrumental in bringing Melanie Klein to London.

JOSEPH, BETTY
Member, BPS; associate of Melanie Klein.

KHAN, MASUD
One of Winnicott's principal associates and explicators; author of several books.

KLEIN, MELANIE
One of the founders of child psychoanalysis; controversial and brilliant theoretician; central figure in the English School of psychoanalysis (as distinguished from the Viennese School, the leader of which was Anna Freud).

KNOPF, MRS. B. J.
Reader who responded to Winnicott's letter to the *Observer* (Letter 88).

KULKA, ANNA M.
Child psychiatrist from Vienna who emigrated to Los Angeles.

LACAN, JACQUES
Controversial French analyst; founder of a school of psychoanalytic thought.

LAING, R. D.
Member, BPS; author of numerous books, including *The Divided Self.*

LANTOS, BARBARA
Member, BPS; associate of Anna Freud.

LIMENTANI, ADAM
Member, BPS; past president, International Psychoanalytical Association.

LOWRY, OLIVER H.
Dean, School of Medicine, Washington University, St. Louis, Missouri.

LURIA, A.R.
Renowned Soviet neuropsychologist.

MAIN, THOMAS
Member, BPS; formerly psychiatrist in charge at Cassel Hospital, West Ham, Surrey.

MCKEITH, RONALD
English pediatrician; president, Royal Society of Medicine, Section on Paediatrics, 1970.

MELTZER, DONALD
American-born Member, BPS; follower of Klein and Bion; author of several books.

MONEY-KYRLE, ROGER
Member, BPS; follower of Klein.

NAGERA, HUMBERTO
Cuban-born child psychoanalyst; associate of Anna Freud.

NELSON, GILLIAN
Reader of *The Child, the Family, and the Outside World.*

PARFITT, D. N.
Australian psychoanalyst.

PELLER, LILI E.
Honorary member, Philadelphia Association for Psychoanalysis.

RAISON, TIMOTHY
Editor of the periodical *The New Society.*

RAPAPORT, DAVID
Distinguished American psychologist and psychoanalyst.

RIES, HANNAH
Member, BPS; follower of Anna Freud; emigrant to United States.

RIVIERE, JOAN
Winnicott's second analyst; close collaborator of Klein; translator of Freud.

RODMAN, F. ROBERT
Los Angeles psychoanalyst.

RODRIGUE, EMILIO
Argentine analyst, trained in London, now practicing in Salvador, Brazil.

ROSENFELD, HERBERT
Member, BPS; associate of Klein; writer on the treatment of psychoses.

RYCROFT, CHARLES F.
Member, BPS (later resigned); writer of articles and books for the psychoanalytic and lay press.

SARGANT, WILLIAM W.
Psychiatrist of organicist orientation.

SCOTT, P. D.
Consultant psychiatrist at Maudsley Hospital; psychiatrist in charge of London County Council Remand Home.

SCOTT, W. CLIFFORD M.
Member, BPS and Canadian Psychoanalytic Society; friend of Winnicott's.

SEGAL, HANNA
Distinguished member of the BPS; one of Melanie Klein's leading disciples.

SHARPE, ELLA
Member, BPS; author of books on technique and dream analysis.

SMIRNOFF, VICTOR
Member, Association Psychoanalytique de France.

SPENCE, MARJORIE
Reader of *The Child, the Family, and the Outside World.*

SPOCK, BENJAMIN
Well-known American pediatrician; author of *Baby and Child Care.*

STIERLIN, HELM
Psychoanalyst of Washington, D.C., now of Heidelberg, West Germany.

STONE, L. JOSEPH
Professor, Vassar College.

STONE, MARJORIE
Manufacturer of toys.

STORR, CHARLES ANTHONY
Distinguished British psychologist, psychoanalyst, and author.

STRACHEY, JAMES
Winnicott's first analyst; translator of Freud.

SZASZ, THOMAS
American analyst; author of *The Myth of Mental Illness* and other polemical works.

THORNER, HANS
Member, BPS.

TIZARD, J. P. M.
Professor of Paediatrics Emeritus at Oxford; old friend of Winnicott's.

TOD, ROBERT
Friend of Winnicott and his wife, Clare; Winnicott wrote a preface to Tod's book about delinquency.

TORRIE, MARGARET
Wife of a friend of Winnicott's.

WILKINSON, AGNES
Consultant psychiatrist to the London School of Economics.

WINNICOTT, VIOLET
Winnicott's sister.

WISDOM, JOHN D.
Professor of philosophy, London School of Economics; past president and honorary fellow, Society for Psychosomatic Research; formerly a member of the BPS.

Index